IMAGES
of Sport

CASTLEFORD
RUGBY LEAGUE

A TWENTIETH CENTURY HISTORY

The captain of Castleford's 1935 cup winning team was international centre
Arthur Atkinson, who was an outstanding player in his day. He retired in 1942
after sixteen years with just one club. Arthur remained a familiar figure in
Castleford and for a number of years worked as a commissionaire at one of the
local cinemas. It was a sad loss to the town as well as the rugby club when he
passed away in 1963. Atkinson remains a Castleford legend to this day. He won
17 international caps, 14 for Yorkshire County and for his club he amassed 431
appearances, scoring 157 tries and kicking 231 goals.

IMAGES
of Sport

CASTLEFORD
RUGBY LEAGUE

A TWENTIETH CENTURY HISTORY

Compiled by
David Smart and Andrew Howard

TEMPUS

First published 2000, reprinted 2003
Copyright © David Smart and Andrew Howard, 2000

Tempus Publishing Limited
The Mill, Brimscombe Port,
Stroud, Gloucestershire, GL5 2QG

ISBN 0 7524 1895 5

Typesetting and origination by
Tempus Publishing Limited
Printed in Great Britain by
Midway Clark Printing, Wiltshire

Also available from Tempus Publishing

Bradford Bulls RLFC	Robert Gate	0 7524 1896 3
Halifax RLFC	Andrew Hardcastle	0 7524 1831 9
Headingley RLFC Voices	Phil Caplan	0 7524 1822 X
Hunslet RLFC	Les Hoole	0 7524 1641 3
Leeds RLFC	Phil Caplan & Les Hoole	0 7524 1140 3
Salford RLFC	Graham Morris	0 7524 1897 1
Sheffield Eagles RLFC	John Cornwell	0 7524 1830 0
St Helens RLFC	Alex Service	0 7524 1883 1
Warrington RLFC	Gary Slater & Eddie Fuller	0 7524 1870 X
Yorkshire Rugby League	Les Hoole	0 7524 1881 5
The Five Nations Story	David Hands	0 7524 1851 3
Yorkshire CCC	Mick Pope	0 7524 0756 2

(all books are 128 page softbacks with the exception of *The Five Nations Story* which is a 176 page hardback with colour illustrations.)

Contents

Lee Crooks takes on the tourists' pack in this 1994 Cas versus Australia clash. A legend in his home town of Hull, Lee's form dipped a little in a spell with Leeds, but his career came right back on track when Castleford paid out £150,000 to sign him in 1990.

Acknowledgements

We are very grateful to the *Pontefract and Castleford Express*, *The Yorkshire Evening Post*, The Rugby Football League, League Express Publications, Malcolm Billingham, Andrew Box, George Claughton, Robert Gate, Mick Hollinworth, Gordon Howard, Sig Kasatkin, Steve Parker, Cyril Roberts, Barney Amesbury, J.W. 'Bill' Spedding and Castleford Tigers RLFC for allowing us the use of their material in putting this book together.

The exact origins of some photographs are unknown. If any copyrights have been infringed there has been no deliberate intent to do so. We would also like to acknowledge those unknown photographers whose images have survived the ravages of time to grace this book.

Introduction

Despite laying claim to being the birthplace of world renowned sculptor Henry Moore, not to mention the world's most famous football pools winner in Viv Nicholson, there is little doubt that in most people's minds the West Yorkshire town of Castleford is synonymous with the game of Rugby League.

Elevated to senior Rugby League status in 1926 the club has had its thin times, but the highs have certainly outweighed those and since the early 1960s, if not always winning trophies, Castleford have never been far away from honours. Although priding itself on representing a small tight-knit community, Castleford's appeal extends far beyond local boundaries and the club have taken great pride in belying the small town image that others would promote – usually by bettering supposed 'bigger' rivals. The cups have provided many moments of glory and joy, sometimes when the league position has not been too good, whilst a lot of pleasure has often come from winning matches that might not in themselves have been vital, but ones that no one expected them to – Cas have always delighted in proving the pundits wrong. There were fears for the club in the new world of Super League, particularly when some seemed intent upon sacrificing the games heartland rather than adding to it, in a move to big city clubs. Again though, Castleford confounded the critics and after some teething problems have positively thrived to the point where they were voted Club of the Year for 1999.

As a lifelong supporter and, latterly, with a more active involvement as the club's official programme editor, I have thoroughly enjoyed my association with Castleford even though there have been days of despair when I wished that I had found another interest. The bug bit me very early though, and when balancing the good days with the bad, they come out in the black. Andrew Howard, who did a terrific job in tracking down many of the photographs for this book, is also a lifelong supporter (although I should add that that life is somewhat shorter than my own!) but he too was bitten by the bug. I have no doubt that people develop similar affinities with other clubs, but somehow Castleford seem special. I hope this book conveys just a little of that.

David Smart

A typical rampaging run from prop forward Kevin Ward, this time against Bradford in the 1987 Yorkshire Cup final. Ward was a big Castleford favourite, making over 300 appearances for the club from 1978 to 1990.

One
The Early Years
1926-1939

Although a Castleford club was generally thought to have been founded in 1896, the present club wasn't formed until 1912, and admission to the senior ranks of the Northern Rugby Football League didn't come until 1926. Before their elevation, Castleford played in the Yorkshire Senior Competition for four seasons. This team photograph features the line-up from one such term, in 1924/25. Among those in the photograph are George 'Gagger' Hinton (in the middle of the back row), John 'Lina' Wilson (first on the left, middle row) and Tommy Needham (first on the left, front row). Clearly unusual nicknames were the order of the day at the time.

Photo. " Express " Series, Ltd.

raining began on Tuesday evening of Castleford Rugby League Club, on the und in Lock Lane, and our photoph, taken on that occasion, shows en of the players who have been ed on for the season, including a ber of the new players who have been ared. The club has now realised its cherished ambition to play in the by League, and their programme ns a month hence at Hull. The Lock e enclosure is to be used for the first son, after which it is expected that club will remove to the Wheldon ld ground, which they have acquired. ood deal of work has been put in on ground, and the turf on the playing was looking in fine condition on sday.

he names of the players show 1 above as follows:—Top row (left to right): p (wing three-quarter), Taylor tre three-quarter). Rathuss (stand-off

half-back), Hobson (forward), H. Hudson (wing three-quarter), Renton (forward), Freeman (centre three-quarter).

Bottom Row: Skelton (wing three-quarter), Sherwood (forward), Thompson (wing three-quarter), Russell (forward), Plimmer (forward), Needham (scrummage half-back), Mattick (stand-off half), and Dickinson (centre three-quarter). The new players are Taylor and Rathuss, of Goldthorpe; Freeman, of Pontefract: Thompson, of Wakefield Trinity; and Skelton, of Dewsbury.

The Castleford Club was represented at the Rugby League Conference at Bridlington, on Monday and Tuesday last, under the chairmanship of Mr. Geo. Taylor, of the Wigan Club. Various secretaries reported that there appeared to be no uniformity in connexion with Entertainment Tax on season tickets. After an explanation by Mr. Penfold (Castleford) it was resolved that no uni-

form action was possible, and that each club should submit its own case. A rule was passed that visiting clubs took 10 per cent. of the gate receipts, excluding stand and membership charges. This materially helps such clubs as Castleford and Featherstone. Much abuse of the use of complimentary tickets was brought to the notice of the meeting, but on the motion of Mr. Garritty, of Featherstone, seconded by Mr. Penfold, of Castleford, it was decided that the present practice of issuing such tickets remain unaltered, the club secretaries being at the same time responsible for the strict and proper issue of such tickets. The management committee of the Rugby League conveyed to the meeting their ruling that the minimum charge to First League matches should be 1/- for adults; prices for boys and ladies to be left to the discretion of the clubs. Mr. Geo. Taylor (Wigan) was elected President, and Mr. T. Naughton

(Widnes) was elected Secretary for coming year.

Castleford have signed on a new ward in Mack Arnold, of Goole Ru Union Club. His age is 22, height 10in., and weight 13st. He plays sec row or loose forward.

As it is now settled that the All Blo reach England in good time for the ranged fixtures, their visit to Castle is certain on Wednesday, September 22 After the match they will be given welcome at a dinner-ball at the K Ballroom, the occasion being one als commemorate Castleford's election to Rugby League.

One of the most extraordinary feat of the Lock Lane ground is the excell system of drainage. Within an hou the recent storms there was no trace water on the ground. Future weat will have to be abnormally bad to in fere with the carrying out of fixtures.

The league's new boys are pictured here at a training session as they prepared for their first season in the senior ranks in July 1926. A number of new players had been brought in to the club, as is reported on in the accompanying article, which also declared that the admission charge for matches was a minimum of 1 shilling (five pence) for male adults; prices for boys and ladies were at the club's discretion. A further announcement is of a dinner/ball to be held at the Kiosk Ballroom on 22 September 1926, to commemorate Castleford's election to the Rugby League. The team ended their first campaign at the foot of the league – winning just 5 of their 36 matches – but top flight Rugby League was up and running in Castleford. The players in this early training session are, from left to right, back row: Kemp, Taylor, Rathuss, Hobson, Hudson, Renton, Freeman. Front row: Skelton, Sherwood, Thompson, Russell, Plimmer, Needham, Mattick, Dickenson.

The 1927/28 season was a momentous one for the club as they moved from their ground, the Sandy Desert in Lock Lane, to their new ground at Wheldon Road, which remains their home today. The ground was purchased from Castleford Town FC and the first visitors were Huddersfield, who spoilt the party by winning 3-0. The next visitors to the new ground were Dewsbury and on this occasion Cas did get a win. In this team picture Arthur Atkinson is second from the left on the back row, with the front row comprised of Harry Russell, Jim Nash, Bill Hargrave, Jim Trevis, Jim Bacon and Bob Nicholls.

The team before an away fixture with Leeds in 1928, one of the earliest such fixtures, in what has become a very keenly-contested derby match. The Cas line-up features, from left to right, back row: Plimmer, Gledhill, Gorman, Powell, Wormold, Russell, (unknown), Devonshire, Hall. Front row: Atkinson, Asquith, Chapman, Hargrave.

Castleford's third campaign in the league, 1928/29, was to be their best to date and it was almost capped by a place in the 1929 Challenge Cup final, the very first to be held at Wembley Stadium. Unfortunately, Dewsbury thwarted those ambitions at the semi-final stage. The players in this shot are, from left to right, back row: Tommy Needham, Jack Wormold, Bob Nicholls, Fred Carter, Bill Renton, Dick Walton, Arthur Sherwood. Front row: Harold Chapman, Bill Asquith, Arthur Atkinson, Bill Hargrave, Edwin Jones, Jim Trevis.

By 1931/32 the club was still coming to terms with the league and finished twenty-second, but again they fared better in the cup, reaching the quarter-final stage. From left to right, back row: Arthur Sherwood, Dick Walton, Arthur Atkinson, Harry Russell, Billy James, Ken Jubb, George Lewis, Cliff Harling. Front row: Albert McGonigle, Tommy Askin, Wilson Hall, Billy Davies, Joe Malkin. George Lewis served the club for many years and kicked 384 goals in well over 300 appearances.

Season 1932/33 proved to be a momentous one as it brought Castleford their first trophy as a senior club when they took the Yorkshire League. This trophy was won by winning what was, in effect, a league within a league. Points accrued throughout the campaign, against those sides from your own county in the regular scheduled fixture lists, produced Yorkshire and Lancashire league tables which were published alongside the full league table. In addition to the overall Championship trophy, separate cups were awarded to the winners of each league. Pictured with the Yorkshire trophy are, from left to right, back row: F. Briggs (director), Haley, A. Smith (director), A. Askin, Sherwood, Taylor, Smith, Jubb, Russell, H. Atkins (director), T. Appleyard (director), Capt. J.A. Pickles (club secretary). Middle row: W. Smith (director), T.C. Askin, Lewis, Atkinson, G. Shaw (chairman), James, Hoult, Knowles, Billy Rhodes (coach). Front row: Davies, Hall.

On 27 September 1933 an Australian touring party made their first-ever visit to Castleford. The tourists, on their fifth tour to Britain, recorded an emphatic 39-6 win over the home side, but were to lose the Test series 3-0. Both sides were lined up together for this historic photograph before the match. The Castleford side that took on the Aussies was comprised of: Pollitt (who kicked three goals), Askin, Lewis, James, Johnson, Davies, Hall, Walton, Haley, Hand, Smith, Russell, Young.

CLE, THURSDAY, SEPTEMBER 28, 1933

TEAM CHANGES

CASTLEFORD'S HANDICAP

Heroic But Hopeless Battle Against Clever Tourists

By CENTRE

Castleford .... 6pts. Australians .... 39pts.

CASTLEFORD laboured under difficulties in their match with the Australians.

In addition to having Atkinson—who has been taken to a nursing home at Pontefract with a severe attack of tonsilitis—and Taylor absent, they also had the misfortune to lose the services of Young, their loose forward, 20 minutes after the start.

It would have been difficult for them to have won in any circumstance. The odds were against them, and the score of six goals and nine tries (39 points) to three goal (6 points) scarcely does justice to their fortitude.

TRIBUTE TO DEFENCE

While their play and skill was incomparable with that of the tourists, I must pay tribute to the home side's defence in spite of the score, and incidentally in doing so, I extend compliments to the tourists' power in attack.

Though the score against them was heavy I found little to criticise Castleford upon. Young Pollitt, at full-back, who was playing in his third match, was uncertain, but he is player of promise.

The Australians' greater mobility was perhaps their best asset, though the quickness with which they handled the ball and supported each other in attack proved more than Castleford were capable of stemming or even copying.

Again must I sing the praises of Thicknesse for scrum-half play. We have never seen a better player from overseas.

Ridley enjoyed another triumph in this his 10th successive match and no forward—and there were many good ones—did more genuinely hard work in a vigorous duel than

the veteran, Madsen, who on this occasion had the honour of captaining the team.

The return of C. Pearce to play as a centre, I think, definitely established the fact that he is of greater use to his side in the middle than on the wing.

He crossed the Castleford line from a movement originating from the starting kick, but the final transfer was forward. Nevertheless, the Tourists were two points up before the game was a minute old. Brown placing a penalty goal.

This excellent centre, who on this occasion played on the left with Neumann, also kicked goals from tries scored by Ridley and Smith, which gave the Tourists an interval lead of 12-0.

Ridley beat two opponents and swerved past Pollitt for his try and the full-back's effort was the culmination of a round of short, sharp passing on the right wing.

The seven tries obtained in the second half were credited to Ridley (2), Pugg, Thicknesse, Gibbs, O'Connor and Brown. The latter player kicked a penalty goal and improved two of the tries. Pollitt kicked three goals for Castleford.

Castleford.—Pollitt; Askin (T.), Lewis, James, Johnson; Davies, Hall; Walton (R.), Haley, Hand, Smith (F.), Russell, Younger.

Australians.—Smith; Ridley, Pearce (C.), Brown, Neumann; Doonar, Thicknesse; Madden, Dempsey, Curran, Gibbs, O'Connor, Prigg.

As the match report outlines, Castleford tried hard against the 1933 Aussie tourists, and the absence of star man Arthur Atkinson through illness must have been a big blow. The young full-back John Pollitt was picked out for a special mention. He was playing in only his third match and showing 'promise', but he only went on to play a further 28 first team games in his four years with the club. The Australian star man was obviously their scrum-half Thicknesse, not the first Aussie number seven to torment British opposition.

Two of Castleford's finest servants before the Second World War were Harold Haley and Jimmy Crossley. Both of these stalwart packmen signed on in the early 1930s and went on to give long and distinguished service to the club. The duo were to play their part in the 1935 cup winning team. Haley, who also figured in the 1939 Championship final side, was born within a stride of the club's ground, and represented Yorkshire in his hooking role. Crossley was a back row forward. They both spent sixteen years at Cas, Haley recording 338 and Crossley 261 appearances. Jim Crossley remained a well-known and popular figure for many years as a local publican.

Another tremendous servant to the Castleford club was centre Jim Croston. Although he had been born in Wigan, Croston lived in Dublin in his youth, as his mother's roots lay there. After joining the British Army, he played Rugby Union and it was through one Forces match that, along with another capture Ted Saddler, he came to the notice of the Castleford club secretary, former military man Captain James Pickles. He was duly signed and over the next 12 years made 283 appearances for Castleford, scoring 150 tries and 52 goals. A tremendous tackler, Croston also represented his country on 7 occasions and his county, Lancashire, 8 times. He won a cup winners' medal for Cas in 1935 and in 1946, having transferred to Wakefield Trinity as player-coach, went on to win a second.

CASTLEFORD DEFEAT BARROW IN CUP SEMI-FINAL

Only nine years after their entry to the League, Castleford fought their way to Wembley in the Rugby League Challenge Cup final. On route they had defeated amateur side Astley and Tyldesley Collieries and then Liverpool Stanley in the first two rounds. In the quarter-final, Hunslet were defeated 10-3 before a record home crowd of 25,499. At the semi-final stage Cas faced Barrow at the Swinton ground, Station Road. They were determined not to let this opportunity slip and Barrow were defeated by 11 points to 5, with tries from Askin, Croston and Knowles and a Lewis goal, as this *Sunday Graphic* feature illustrates.

17

Castleford travelled to London to face Huddersfield, one of the code's best and longest established sides, but triumphed 11 points to 8 to bring the town its first major trophy. This action shot from the Wembley final features two of the Huddersfield side (in the dark jerseys) apparently admiring a tackle by one of their team-mates, whilst Castleford's Tommy Askin looks on. Askin was a former Featherstone and Leeds player who had won international honours before joining the club. In almost 200 appearances for Cas he scored 64 tries.

Scrum-half Les 'Juicy' Adams breaks from the scrum in this action shot from Wembley in 1935. Adams had already won cup winners' medals with Leeds in 1932 and Huddersfield in 1933. He went on to make 6 appearances for Yorkshire and won 2 England caps whilst with Cas, but sadly was a casualty of the Second World War.

18

Castleford's points in their first Wembley final came through tries by Bernard Cunniffe, Tommy Askin and Les Adams, with Arthur Atkinson kicking a goal. A crowd of 39,000 watched the match and saw skipper Arthur Atkinson make an uncharacteristic early error, knocking on with the tryline begging, and then missing a penalty. However, he and his side recovered from these setbacks to take the lead and, despite a strong Huddersfield fightback and nervous finale, held on to deservedly clinch the cup. The trials and tribulations are forgotten as Arthur Atkinson receives the cup for Castleford from Mr J. Lewthwaite, the Rugby League's chairman.

Winning skipper Arthur Atkinson is chaired from the Wembley arena by two of his team's heroes, props Tommy Taylor and Pat McManus. There were no substitutes in those days, but travelling reserve Donald Knowles in his cup final suit is alongside, sharing in the celebrations. The forward duo of Taylor and McManus gave long and loyal service to the Castleford club, making 389 and 296 appearances respectively.

The actual cover of the 1935 Cup final programme was, in part, printed in silver to mark the occasion of the Silver Jubilee of King George V and Queen Mary – although the royal couple were not in attendance at the match. However, the French international squad were guests at the Wembley final, having travelled to England to play in a special match to commemorate the Jubilee.

Back home and flanked by the club's directors and officials, the cup winners proudly pose with their trophy. The line-up of the thirteen who won on the day (and the travelling reserve Donald Knowles) is, from left to right, middle row: Frank Smith, Tommy Taylor, Ted Sadler, Knowles, Pat McManus. Front row: Bernard Cunniffe, George Lewis, Jimmy Croston, Arthur Atkinson, Tommy Askin, Harold Haley, Jim Crossley. Kneeling: Les Adams, Billy Davies.

Castleford's second major final came in 1939, when they reached the Championship final. After finishing second in the league, they defeated Halifax in the top four play-off semi-final to win a place in the final at Maine Road, the home of Manchester City soccer club. Before the match, the players had a look at this famous old ground and, with some of his colleagues and club chairman Gideon Shaw looking on, second row forward Ted Sadler tests the posts for strength.

A then world record Rugby League crowd of 69,504 gathered at Maine Road for the Championship final to watch Cas take on Salford. With regular skipper Arthur Atkinson an absentee, Les Adams led the side out – but it was not to be their day. With tries from Jimmy Robinson and Fred Brindle, Castleford were holding a 6-5 lead as the game drew to its close, but they were denied victory when Salford grabbed a late try (after a fortuitous bounce) to triumph 8-6.

Winger Reg Lloyd finds himself crossing the touchline as Salford's Barney Hudson gives chase in the 1939 Championship final. Lloyd is one of only a few Castleford players to have represented Wales, winning 7 caps for his country. Signed from Keighley, he made 248 appearances in a thirteen-year spell at the club.

More action from the 1939 final, as one of Castleford's stars in the match, loose forward Fred Brindle, moves in to cover Salford's Kenny. Brindle brought some valuable experience to the side when he was signed in 1937, having had spells with Hull KR, Huddersfield and Halifax.

Two
The Fallow Years
1940-1959

This 1946/47 line-up won a rare victory at Headingley when they defeated Leeds 11-8 in the Yorkshire Cup first round, first leg. From left to right, back row: Pat McManus, Harold Fox, Harold Haley, Eddie Lavender, Geoff Briggs, Ron Copley, Charlie Staines. Front row: Eric Jones, Fred Church, Jim Robinson, George Langfield, Reg Lloyd, Norman Guest.

This cartoon drawing from 1947 featured some of the key players and officials of the day. One of those represented was George Langfield, a local lad who had walked into the club and asked for a trial. Within weeks he was embarking on a career with Cas that saw him play in 228 matches, scoring 391 goals and 62 tries before his transfer to St Helens took him to even greater success.

Typical of the official programme of the time was this 1948/49 edition. The match was against Bradford Northern and Cas lost 5-11. Beyond advertisements, the contents were limited to the teams and just one half page of 'Club Gossip'. This reflected on the team's loss of form and the need to draft in some younger blood as some of the players were 'getting on in years'.

CASTLEFORD. R.L.F.C.
TEAM v WIGAN at WHELDON ROAD. FEB 14ᵗʰ/48

A big home crowd looks forward to this Castleford side taking on Wigan in February 1948, in a Challenge Cup first round, second leg tie. Having lost the first leg at Wigan 27-0, Cas had an awful lot to do and, although they gave an improved performance, they went down 7-19. The photograph shows the team – for whom Norman Guest scored a try and a goal and Des Foreman a goal – with their backs to Wheldon Road and the Wheldale Hotel (before that part of the ground was covered). Later in the same year, Castleford reached their first Yorkshire Cup final, beating Bramley, Hull and Wakefield along the way. Their opponents in the final were Bradford Northern, with the match taking place at Headingley. Cas were unable to clinch the trophy, eventually losing 9-18, with the points coming from a Des Foreman try and goals from Foreman, Charlie Staines and George Langfield. Third from the right, in the back row of this team shot is Jimmy Crossley, who appeared in the 1935 Wembley victory. The 1948/49 season was his last campaign in the Cas pack, severing the final link in terms of players, with the cup final team.

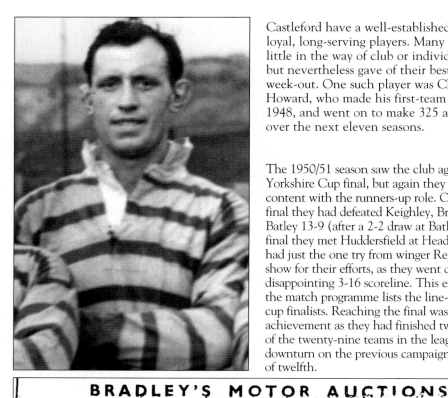

Castleford have a well-established tradition of loyal, long-serving players. Many won precious little in the way of club or individual honours, but nevertheless gave of their best week-in week-out. One such player was Charlie Howard, who made his first-team debut in 1948, and went on to make 325 appearances over the next eleven seasons.

The 1950/51 season saw the club again reach the Yorkshire Cup final, but again they had to be content with the runners-up role. On route to the final they had defeated Keighley, Bradford and Batley 13-9 (after a 2-2 draw at Batley). In the final they met Huddersfield at Headingley, but had just the one try from winger Reg Lloyd to show for their efforts, as they went down by a disappointing 3-16 scoreline. This extract from the match programme lists the line-ups for the cup finalists. Reaching the final was quite an achievement as they had finished twenty-fifth out of the twenty-nine teams in the league – a real downturn on the previous campaign's final placing of twelfth.

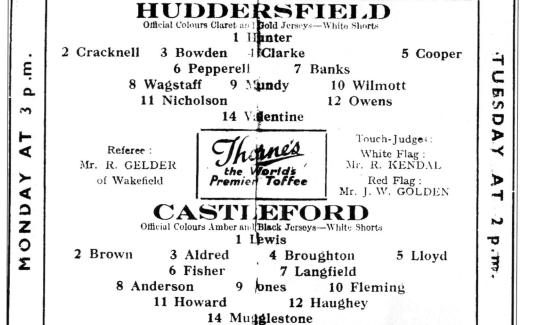

BRADLEY'S MOTOR AUCTIONS

MONDAY AT 3 p.m.

TUESDAY AT 2 p.m.

HUDDERSFIELD
Official Colours Claret and Gold Jerseys—White Shorts

1 Hunter

2 Cracknell   3 Bowden   4 Clarke   5 Cooper

6 Pepperell   7 Banks

8 Wagstaff   9 Mundy   10 Wilmott

11 Nicholson   12 Owens

14 Valentine

Referee :
Mr. R. GELDER
of Wakefield

*Thorne's
the World's
Premier Toffee*

Touch-Judges :
White Flag :
Mr. R. KENDAL
Red Flag :
Mr. J. W. GOLDEN

CASTLEFORD
Official Colours Amber and Black Jerseys—White Shorts

1 Lewis

2 Brown   3 Aldred   4 Broughton   5 Lloyd

6 Fisher   7 Langfield

8 Anderson   9 Jones   10 Fleming

11 Howard   12 Haughey

14 Mugglestone

110, GELDERD ROAD LEEDS 12   Tel. 23014

A new signing in 1951 was local boy Albert Lunn. An Airedale Juniors player, Albert was to become one of the club's most distinguished servants, over a twelve-year playing career (largely at full-back) and then later as the club's groundsman. In both of these roles, Albert never let the side down. His playing debut came against the now defunct Belle Vue Rangers, the first of 363 appearances in which he kicked 875 goals. Local artist J.W. Spedding drew this sketch, marking Lunn's time at the club as both player and staff.

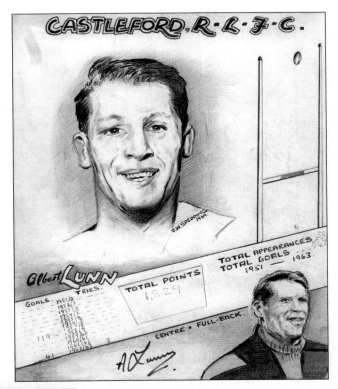

Individual representative honours for Castleford players were very rare during the 1950s, as the club generally struggled in the league. A couple of players did win Yorkshire caps though, one being classy centre Denzil Webster. Webster scored 63 tries in just 98 appearances for Cas, winning a Yorkshire County cap and a winners' medal against Cumberland at Odsal in 1955.

The 1950s were generally a very thin time for Castleford. The 1956/57 season was typical, with just 11 victories in their 38 fixtures, leaving them twenty-fifth in a league of thirty clubs. Injuries bit hard and no fewer than nineteen players made their debut through the campaign. From left to right, back row: Geoff Ward, Harry Thornley, John Sheridan, Charlie Howard, Frank East, Cliff Burton, Fred Ward, Arthur Wilmot. Front row: Ken Hindley, Albert Lunn, Ron Evans, Ken Pye, Jack Barnes, Barry Walsh. Ken Pye was another great servant to the club. His thirteen-year career with Cas took him from playing scrum-half, through the back row and eventually to prop forward. Before his transfer to Keighley in 1963, Pye played 344 matches in the black and amber and scored 70 tries.

John Sheridan had signed for Cas in the mid-1950s and, as a centre and then later a loose forward, gave outstanding service to the club in over 300 appearances. Many felt that at a more fashionable and successful club he could have won representative honours. Having retired as a player, he continued to serve the club well for a number of years in developing young talent as the second team coach.

The 1958/59 term was another thin time for the club's faithful followers, with another poor league campaign and early knock-outs in the cup competitions. However, during the season, although not in this line-up, two young stars by the names of Alan Hardisty and Keith Hepworth emerged to signal the beginning of a very significant shift in the club's fortunes. From left to right, back row: Colin Taylor, Charles Wright, Charlie Howard, Geoff Ward, Jack Hirst, Albert Tonkinson, Cliff Burton, John Sheridan, Frank East. Front row: Ian Corban, Albert Lunn, Ron Evans, Barry Walsh, Colin Battye, Ken Pye.

As the 1950s drew to a close, Castleford supporters witnessed the emergence of the first batch of highly talented local youngsters who were to serve the club so well and change its fortunes. Two of these already mentioned, half-backs and schoolboy pals Alan Hardisty and Keith Hepworth, shone like beacons and were to prove the catalyst for the good times ahead. The legendary Alan Hardisty made his debut at Keighley in September 1958. He was only just seventeen but his class was immediately apparent. It wasn't too long before he was followed into the first team by his future 'H-Bombs' half-back partner Keith Hepworth – another seventeen year old, who made his first team debut at Huddersfield in April 1959.

Three
The Castleford Renaissance
1960-1974

Captain Alan Hardisty collects the 1969 Challenge Cup on an afternoon at Wembley that sealed his side's prominence in the game.

When the 1961 New Zealand tourists visited this country, a historic link between Castleford and their neighbours and rivals Featherstone was forged. The Kiwis couldn't play all of the sides in the league and, rather than play just a small hand-picked selection, in a number of their tour fixtures they played combined teams. One of those combinations was a Castleford and Featherstone XIII. The match took place at Wheldon Road and, of the thirteen on duty, five players were from Cas – Albert Lunn, Geoff Ward, Colin Battye, Alan Hardisty and John Sheridan – and eight from Featherstone. The combined team, who played in red jerseys, looked good on paper, but weren't strong enough for their overseas visitors, who triumphed 31-20. The official programme speculated on whether this temporary merger might be a prelude to a permanent banding together of the two clubs, a concept that was to be raised again some thirty-five years later when the Super League was launched. Thankfully, on neither occasion was the suggestion taken forward.

Hopes were high that a mixed season in 1961/62 might have ended in cup glory for Cas. However, Huddersfield barred their path in the quarter-final, which saw over 16,000 spectators gather at Wheldon Lane for this eagerly awaited clash. Home full-back Albert Lunn's two penalties were matched by his opposite number Frank Dyson, as the match ended 4-4. The replay took place four days later at Fartown, but all Cas had to show was another two Lunn penalties as Huddersfield won 10-4.

In the summer of 1962, local centre Peter Small had become Castleford's first Great Britain tourist since Arthur Atkinson in 1936. Small was an accomplished centre (and, later, back row forward) who made over 300 appearances for the club, but his selection caused something of a surprise at the time. He proved his worth though by having a successful tour and won a cap in the Second Test against New Zealand in Auckland, scoring one of the Great Britain tries. Although Small never added to this one cap, he did represent the Yorkshire county side against Australia in 1967, by which time he had made the switch to second row.

Although the shoots were starting to show at the end of the 1950s, Castleford's renaissance was to be confirmed as the next decade unfolded. This team photograph from the 1962/63 season, when fourth place in the First Division made Cas the highest placed Yorkshire side, features four future Great Britain internationals in Alan Hardisty, Keith Hepworth, Bill Bryant and Johnny Ward. The line-up is, from left to right, back row: Albert Tonkinson, Jack Hirst, Keith Slatter, Bryant, John Walker, John Sheridan, Peter Small, Harry Street (coach). Front row: Trevor Bedford, Ward, Hepworth, Hardisty, Eric Nowell, Jack Gamble, Keith Howe, Geoff Ward.

Keith Howe joined Cas from Old Rodillians, a Rugby Union club comprised of the old boys of Rothwell Grammar School, and the three-quarter soon showed an eye for the tryline. On his debut against Workington in May 1963 he scored two tries, eventually going on to amass 109 in 167 appearances for the club. In season 1963/64 he broke the club's long established tries in a season record when he notched 36 touchdowns at the rate of almost a try a match in 38 appearances.

Although dropping a couple of places in 1963/64 to sixth spot in the First Division, Castleford did do better in the cup competitions. They reached the Challenge Cup semi-final and, having drawn with Widnes at Swinton, suffered the bitter disappointment of a 5-7 replay defeat before a packed crowd of 28,700 at Wakefield's Belle Vue ground. This squad lined up before one of the home matches in the campaign, from left to right, back row: Len Garbett (club secretary), John Sheridan, Jack Hirst, Bill Bryant, Doug Walton, Geoff Ward, John Walker, Ken Foulkes, Peter Small, Frank Smith, Harry Street (coach). Front row: Keith Howe, Johnny Ward, Derek Edwards, Alan Hardisty, H.H. Clarkson (chairman), Keith Hepworth, Roy Bell, John Clark.

A different jersey style for the Castleford team, who travelled to Wakefield for a local derby clash in January 1964. The result was a narrow defeat for this Cas line-up, from left to right, back row: John Walker, Bill Bryant, Roy Bell, Albert Tonkinson, Jack Hirst, Andy Johnson, Frank Smith. Front row: Jack Gamble, Derek Edwards, John Ward, Alan Hardisty, Keith Hepworth, Keith Howe.

Cas also reached the Eastern Division Championship final in 1964, which took place at Huddersfield's Fartown ground. This competition was supplementary to the two divisionial set-up. It was mirrored by a Western Division, featuring clubs from both divisions facing clubs from their respective sides of the Pennines. The official programme carried a design that collectors became very familiar with, as the Rugby League were to use it for their big match covers for a number of years. Castleford lost the final 12-20 to Halifax, with winger Keith Howe gaining some consolation in scoring a try that contributed to his record-breaking 36 for the season.

THE RUGBY FOOTBALL LEAGUE

EAST REGION CHAMPIONSHIP FINAL

CASTLEFORD v. HALIFAX

SATURDAY
MAY 23rd
1964

At
FARTOWN
HUDDERSFIELD

Kick-off 3.0 p.m.

OFFICIAL SOUVENIR PROGRAMME - Price 1/-

Silverware was won in 1964/65 when the club took the Yorkshire League and finished third in the overall Championship table, which was now back to one league. Players Ron Willett, Trevor Bedford, John Taylor, Colin Battye, John Walker, Abe Terry, Doug Walton, Clive Dickenson, Alan Hardisty and Keith Hepworth are pictured here gathering round the Yorkshire League trophy. Doug Walton, who is almost hidden by the cup, was a local player who burst onto the scene in a big way and represented Great Britain against France in 1965, at just eighteen years of age. Unfortunately injuries blighted Doug's career and he was unable to fulfil that early promise.

The board and club officials share in the team's glory after a successful 1964/65 campaign. The players and coach featured are, from left to right, back row: Clive Dickinson, Barry Charlesworth, Pete Barton, John Walker. Middle row: Doug Walton, Abe Terry, Bill Bryant, Maurice Williams, Keith Howe, George Clinton (coach). Front row: Ron Willett, Malcolm Battye, Colin Battye, Alan Hardisty, Keith Hepworth, Derek Edwards, Peter Small.

Keith Howe is unable to stop the home side scoring in this match against Halifax at Thrum Hall during January 1965. Castleford lost 3-23, with their solitary try coming from Jack Gamble (who was later to join Halifax). Howe's three-quarter colleagues, Peter Small and Geoff Ward, are also on the scene, but all in vain.

In 1965/66 the BBC, looking for a midweek sports programme for their second channel, introduced the BBC2 Floodlit Trophy Competition. Matches were played on midweek evenings and, as such, were limited to those clubs with floodlights, an asset not held by all at the time. Thankfully, Castleford, having installed them that very season, were eligible to enter – and this was to prove a very successful competition for the club. The final was not held on neutral territory and a trip to Knowsley Road to face St Helens was a daunting task. Defences won the day but thanks to two Ron Willett goals, Cas won the trophy 4 points to nil. Skipper Alan Hardisty holds the Floodlit Trophy aloft, chaired by Peter Small and Colin Battye, with young protégé Roger Millward in front.

Alan Hardisty, having showered and changed, is still celebrating with his team-mates in the dressing room after the 1965/66 Floodlit Trophy win. Joining the players in their moment of glory is club chairman Ron Simpson.

Castleford won the new floodlit competition for the first three years, following its introduction into the Rugby League calendar. In 1966/67 they beat Swinton in the final 7-2 at home with a Jack Austin try and goals from Ron Willett and Keith Hepworth. The following year they completed the hat-trick when they defeated Leigh 8-5 at Headingley. The team and the club's board of directors are pictured here with the Floodlit Trophy after their third successive triumph.

Keith Hepworth leads the side out for a match at Headingley against Leeds in August 1966. For many years, a trip to the North Leeds ground usually ended in defeat for Castleford, and this match was no exception as they went down 2-23. 'Heppy' led the side in the absence of his half-back partner Alan Hardisty, although they were rarely parted in their time at the club – nor indeed were they when they left, as they both enjoyed a spell at Leeds. Scrum-half Hepworth had a tremendous work rate and complemented Hardisty's flair. Not that 'Heppy' couldn't attack – he notched 66 tries in his 329 Castleford appearances. He also played 11 times for Great Britain and 5 times for Yorkshire County. The combination of Hardisty and Hepworth seemed a match made in heaven and Castleford fans who saw them at their peak will have seen few, if any, better pairings.

The legendary Malcolm Reilly stepping out behind Dennis Hartley on his Castleford debut, which came in the centre position at Hunslet in September 1967. Although he played rugby at school, as a teenager Reilly was a keen local amateur football player with Kippax. One Saturday afternoon his side's soccer match was postponed and he opted to play for the local Rugby League team, whose game was going ahead. The rest, as they say, is history and the career of Malcolm Reilly OBE was underway.

Ron Hill, who signed for Castleford from the Cardiff Rugby Union club, has to leave the field early in this match at Hunslet in September 1967. The old Parkside ground certainly wasn't a happy place for Hill – the goal-kicking full-back made his Castleford debut there in 1965 and suffered a broken jaw. Hill went on to play in 83 matches and kicked 159 goals, before switching to Salford, who he played for against Castleford in the 1969 cup final.

Malcolm Reilly on his way to a try at York in January 1968. It was one of a brace scored by the young loose forward, who had quickly made his mark in the game and found his best position. In this match his side completed a very comfortable 40 points to 19 league victory over the Minstermen.

Promising young centre Ian Stenton was another Cas scorer in the January 1968 win over York. Another of the many local junior products who made good, Stenton went on to win a cup winners' medal and represented the Yorkshire County side.

Second rower Bill Bryant is tackled by the Hull KR defenders in his testimonial match in August 1968, which ended as a 22-22 draw. Bryant, or 'Big Bill' as he was popularly known, was a Normanton product who, at his best, was one of the game's top back rowers. He won 5 Great Britain caps, with injuries costing him many more. He signed as a sixteen year old in 1957 and for many years was the backbone of the pack, before the signing of Dennis Hartley and the emergence of young stars such as Malcolm Reilly and Brian Lockwood. By this time injuries were taking their toll and tragically cost him the chance of well-deserved cup success in 1969. He made 253 appearances and was a regular try scorer (for a forward) with 75 in his career.

With a new coach, Derek Turner, and a team that was looking ever more impressive, hopes were high as the 1968/69 season got underway. Those hopes were to be largely realised by this line-up. From left to right, back row: Trevor Briggs, Malcolm Reilly, Brian Lockwood, Dennis Hartley, Frank Fox, Dennis Harris, Alan Lowndes. Front row: Clive Dickinson, Derek Edwards, Tony Thomas, Alan Hardisty, Keith Hepworth, John Ward, Keith Howe, Trevor Bedford.

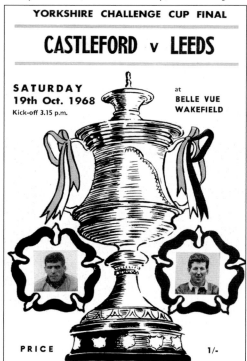

Early in the 1968/69 season, Castleford won through to their first Yorkshire Cup final for many years. Under their new coach, a hard fought semi-final at Odsal saw Bradford beaten by just 16 points to 15, winning Cas the right of a final place against Leeds at Wakefield's Belle Vue ground. On the day though, a strong Leeds side were too good and won the match 22-11. These two sides were to figure in many epic clashes over the next few years, often in key matches.

This J.W. Spedding sketch captures prop Dennis Hartley, who was signed from Hunslet in 1966. Dennis was a tremendous buy for the club and added necessary steel. He really came into his own as Cas began to progress and in the big matches his contribution was invaluable. Dennis played 268 matches for the club and was then on the coaching staff for many years. A truly loyal servant of Castleford, Dennis also won 9 Great Britain caps.

The first step on the road to Wembley in 1969 was at Hunslet. The home side gave a good account of themselves in front of a packed Parkside crowd. Mick Redfearn – more noted for his kicking, with three goals in this match – is pictured adding a try to claim nine points in his side's 19-7 victory.

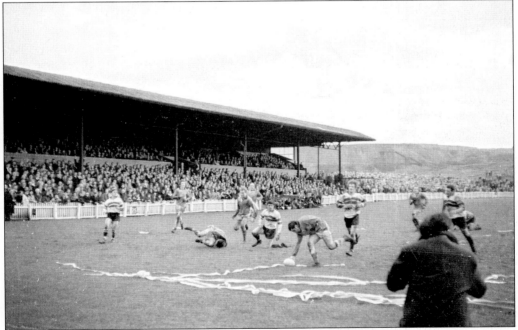

PRICE 5d

YORKSHIRE
EVENING POST

RUGBY LEAGUE SPECIAL

'CAS' FOR THE CUP

SKIPPER ALAN HARDISTY LEADS HIS MEN INTO ACTION AGAINST SALFORD IN THE RUGBY LEAGUE CUP FINAL ON MAY 17th.

Winter Rugby League, and a cold snowy Wheldon Lane, as the groundstaff prepare for the second round of the 1969 Challenge Cup. The bleak February weather didn't stop the match going ahead as the snow was cleared and, whilst it might have been cold on the terraces, it was warm (if not fiery) on the field of play. Castleford hooker Johnny Ward was the star performer, before he and Wigan forward Brian Hogan were dismissed – although he was ultimately celebrating as his side won 12-8.

The *Yorkshire Evening Post* produced a special edition to celebrate Castleford's achievement in reaching the 1969 Challenge Cup final. Despite being pitted against Salford – at the time the code's big money side – the paper were clearly very confident of victory for their local team.

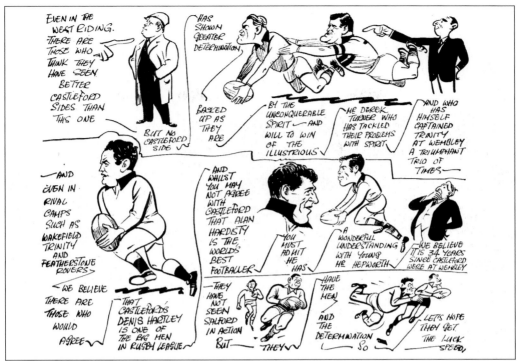

In the *Evening Post* special, cartoonist Speed added his own contribution. The spirit that had shone throughout the cup campaign was an appropriate focus because some of the 'Classy Cas' style – which had won the club many friends, but not the silverware that it deserved – had to be sacrificed. In the semi-final Cas ground out a win against local rivals Wakefield, with Mick Redfearn's goal-kicking the deciding factor. Redfearn's five goals, added to tries by Alan Hardisty and Trevor Briggs, were too much for Trinity who also scored two tries but the legendary Neil Fox could only add a couple of goals.

Chairman Bill Broxup and skipper Alan Hardisty lead Castleford out at Wembley for the 1969 Challenge Cup final. A sell-out crowd of 98,000 saw a momentous day in the club's history against big-spending Salford. It had been thirty-four years since the club's last trip to Wembley and although Cas had an impressive line-up, they had promised much throughout the 1960s without winning a big prize. That was about to change.

The victorious team hoists captain Alan Hardisty and coach Derek 'Rocky' Turner aloft after their 11-6 Challenge Cup victory over Salford. Hardisty was a tryscorer, along with Keith Howe and Keith Hepworth, whilst Mick Redfearn added a goal. Loose forward Mal Reilly, with a typical rip-roaring display, won the Man of the Match award. Coach Turner, a former playing star at Wakefield, was credited with adding steel to the 'Classy Cas' outfit, who had established a reputation for free-flowing rugby but had missed out on those major trophies.

A very contented-looking Alan Hardisty poses with the Challenge Cup. He had every right to be happy as the star stand-off had played a big part in its return to Castleford for the first time since 1935 (and only the second occasion in the club's history that they had won the trophy).

The cup comes back to Castleford as the 1969 Challenge Cup stars arrive home in the town to a rapturous welcome. Many thousands had followed their team to Wembley and massive crowds awaited their return on an exciting, yet emotional, evening. The coach followed a twelve-mile route through streets lined with fans before reaching their destination at Castleford Boys Secondary School, where a huge crowd had amassed.

Another chance for a pose with the cup as the club's directors gather around the Wembley squad for the formal photograph. From left to right (coach and players only), middle row: Derek Turner, Clive Dickinson, Malcolm Reilly, Brian Lockwood, Dennis Hartley, Frank Fox, Trevor Briggs, Mick Redfearn, Dennis Harris, Derek Edwards. Front row: Keith Howe, Tony Thomas, Alan Hardisty, Keith Hepworth, Alan Lowndes, John Ward.

Having won the Challenge Cup, Cas were in with a chance of the double in 1969, as they had also won through to the Championship final for the first time since 1939. Leeds were their opponents, with the match taking place at Odsal just a week after the Wembley triumph. For a long time in the match it looked as if the trophy cabinet was set to hold the game's two biggest trophies. Sadly, Leeds had other ideas and the dream of a double was cruelly snatched away with the Loiners clinching a narrow 16-14 victory.

The *Yorkshire Evening Post* ran a series of player profiles during the 1969/70 season and most of the Castleford heroes of the day were featured. Brian Lockwood was one such player, a local junior who won district honours at under-17 level and rose to the heights of World Cup glory with Great Britain in 1972. Lockwood started out in the second row before switching to prop and, as well as winning two Challenge Cup winners medals for Castleford, he added to his collection through further Wembley wins with Hull KR and Widnes. He won 7 Great Britain caps, represented Yorkshire on 6 occasions and made 231 appearances for Castleford. Lockwood also spent some time playing in Australia, adding to his reputation in the 'Big League' competition.

RL MEN OF ACTION
—BRIAN LOCKWOOD

Here is another in the popular Evening Post series that features well-known Rugby League players. Readers are invited to apply on the form provided for copies, on art paper, of these fine pictures and autographs. They appear each Monday

One of the iron men in Castleford's highly respected pack is second-row forward BRIAN LOCKWOOD.

A product of the Castleford Junior side, Lockwood is reputed to be " as hard as nails." He has commanded a regular place for the past two seasons.

A notable figure in Castleford's Wembley Cup Final victory over Salford in May, Lockwood won his first Yorkshire cap against Lancashire this season.

RL MEN OF ACTION
—JOHNNY WARD

Here is another in our action-shot series of well-known Rugby League players. Readers are invited to apply on the form provided for copies on art paper of these pictures—and autographs — that appear each Monday in the Evening Post.

One of Rugby League's classiest forwards is Castleford's Johnny Ward (facing camera), who joined the club on a free transfer from Featherstone Rovers.

Ward, who is a licensee at Kippax, started as a hooker and played for Great Britain against Australia at Headingley in 1963; scoring the first try in a 16-7 home victory.

Last season he switched successfully to blind-side prop and won honours again this season playing for England against Wales and France.

Johnny Ward was another player featured in the *Evening Post*'s profiles, but it wasn't long before he was on the move from the club in controversial circumstances. A free transfer signing from neighbours Featherstone, Ward had become an influential member of the Castleford pack as a hooker or prop and won both Great Britain and England international honours. He had rocked the club by asking for a transfer but was persuaded to come off the transfer list a couple of weeks before they set out on the trail to defend the Challenge Cup. However, three days before the cup signing deadline Salford came in with a £6,000 bid which was accepted and Ward was on his way. Club chairman Harry Clarkson quit the board that he had served on for twenty-one years in protest at the decision.

49

A tight fight at Swinton

A pair of pictures bursting with action . . . they were taken by Evening Post cameraman Roy Fox at the R.L. Cup semi-final at Swinton where Castleford beat St. Helens 6-3.

On the right, the keen struggle for a place in the Final at Wembley is summed up in this shot of Castleford scrum-half Hepworth and St. Helens centre Walsh in a face-to-face tussle.

Below: Alan Lowndes bursts through the Saints' defence, but is held inches from the line by Walsh and scrum-half Heaton (No. 7). Castleford, in fact, never succeeded in chalking up a try in this tightly-fought game. Their six points came from three drop goals.

At the semi-final stage of the 1970 Challenge Cup, Castleford were given the tough task of facing St Helens at Swinton's ground, Station Road. Tough as it was, the match was won – although in unusual circumstances. At the time, drop goals were worth two points and Castleford notched three of them through Alan Hardisty, Bill Kirkbride and Malcolm Reilly to give them six points. Saints did cross the line for a try (then worth three points), but just the once, and Cas were back at Wembley on the strength of a 6-3 win.

Speed's cartoon in the *Yorkshire Evening Post* previews the 1970 Challenge Cup final, where Wigan were the opposition. Wigan's kicker Colin Tyrer had a reputation for the time he took over his goal kicks. However, an injury to the full-back, which caused him to leave the action, was to cause far more controversy – Wigan felt that it was as a result of a deliberate foul.

The Castleford cheerleaders prepare for their Wembley appearance. Jeannette Marsh, Josephine Smith, Sandra Gray and Frances Swallow were the lucky girls who were selected at a supporters' club function.

THE RUGBY LEAGUE CHALLENGE CUP COMPETITION

FINAL

SATURDAY, MAY 9, 1970 Kick-off 3p.m.

CASTLEFORD V WIGAN

Official Programme   Two Shillings

EMPIRE **WEMBLEY** STADIUM

As this official programme illustrates, there was no thirty-four year wait this time. Castleford were back at Wembley after just one year following an impressive cup campaign. On route they had accounted for Hull, Barrow, Salford and St Helens in the semi-final. Wigan were the opposition and both teams were packed with top-class international stars, Castleford having had Derek Edwards, Alan Hardisty, Keith Hepworth, Dennis Hartley and Mal Reilly selected for the forthcoming 1970 summer Great Britain tour to Australia and New Zealand.

Malcolm Reilly, typically, in the thick of the action in the 1970 Challenge Cup final. Reilly was by now established as one of the game's biggest stars, but he was just one of what had become an all round strong and tough pack who were able to dominate in the big matches.

Tommy Smales celebrates after his team had retained the Challenge Cup with a 7-2 victory over Wigan. In an often dour and controversial encounter, a try from winger Alan Lowndes and two goals from Mick Redfearn were enough to keep the cup in Castleford, who became only the second side to win two successive Wembley finals. Second row forward Bill Kirkbride, who was a new signing that season, won the Lance Todd Trophy as Man of the Match.

Champagne and milk are both on offer as the 1970 Challenge Cup winners commence the post-match celebrations in the Wembley dressing room. Tryscorer Alan Lowndes looks to have selected the alcoholic option on behalf of his team-mates.

Another triumphant homecoming as the players display the cup to the people of Castleford on their return from Wembley. Again the streets had been packed with well-wishers and it was obvious that, despite winning the cup for a second successive year, no one was getting blasé about it. From left to right: Bill Kirkbride, Ian Stenton, Trevor Briggs (at the back), Mal Reilly, Keith Hepworth, Clive Dickinson, Alan Hardisty, Tony Thomas, Mick Redfearn, Brian Lockwood.

The Pontefract and Castleford Express 1970 cup final report reflects on Castleford's achievement in winning a second successive Challenge Cup, but also on the Tyrer incident.

Cumbrian second row forward Bill Kirkbride joined the club on the eve of the 1969/70 season from Halifax. Within a year he had won a cup winners' medal and the Lance Todd Trophy as Man of the Match in the 1970 Wembley win. However, his time with the club was short and midway through the following term he moved to Salford.

Former Huddersfield and Great Britain star Tommy Smales had just one full season as coach to Castleford, but he led his side to a second successive Wembley triumph in 1970. Smales's appointment tempered the blow of losing Derek Turner who, after his highly successful year with Castleford, had been tempted away to take up the coaching role at Leeds. Smales (right) discusses tactics with skipper Alan Hardisty and long-serving hooker Clive Dickinson. He didn't stay too long, though, departing part way through the 1970/71 season, just seven months after that cup final victory. The team at the time was, tragically, beginning to break up with lots of rumours of discontent in the camp and the confirmed departure for Australia of Malcolm Reilly.

When Tommy Smales left the club in December 1970, Alan Hardisty took up the vacant coach's role, initially continuing to play, before, as the season drew to a close, announcing his retirement as a player to concentrate on his coaching duties. His side just missed out on a third successive Wembley trip after losing 8-19 to Leeds in the semi-final but, to the dismay of Castleford followers, their hero Hardisty was allowed to leave the club at the end of the season. Hardisty is pictured here in that semi-final against Leeds at Odsal attempting to tackle the opposing captain, Syd Hynes. Alan resumed his playing career at Leeds, where he added to the many honours won with Castleford. In his 401 games for Castleford, Hardisty, regarded by many as the club's finest-ever player, scored 206 tries and kicked 120 goals.

The 1971/72 line-up, from left to right, back row: Brian Lockwood, Graham Blakeway, Ian Van Bellen, Alan Ackroyd, Derek Foster, Keith Worsley, Tony Miller, Alan Dickinson. Front row: Gary Stephens, Derek Edwards, Glyn Jones, Dennis Hartley, Alan Lowndes, Steve Norton, Danny Hargrave. This season saw the club make their fourth appearance in a Yorkshire Cup final, but again they lost out. Hull KR were the team who thwarted Castleford's ambitions with a narrow 11-7 victory; Derek Foster with a try and Alan Ackroyd with two goals were the Cas scorers.

Gifts from supporters' organisations to players gaining representative honours added to the achievement. This *Pontefract and Castleford Express* article features Keith Worsley and Steve Norton receiving gifts to mark their selection for Yorkshire and Brian Lockwood to commemorate his Great Britain appearances from the Castleford Rugby League Queen, Noreen Dale. 'Knocker' Norton went on to win many more honours – some were with Cas, but the best years of his career were spent with Hull.

Supporters of Castleford Rugby League Club presented skipper Brian Lockwood with two watches to mark his selection for Great Britain in the last World Cup competition, at a social evening at the Wheldon Road ground on Friday.

To mark their selection for Yorkshire this term, Keith Worsley and Steve Norton also received gifts. Norton was presented with a coffee table and Worsley a transistor radio.

Lockwood received his awards from the Castleford and Knottingley supporters.

In receiving his awards, Lockwood said: — "I would like to thank all supporters for their generosity in making these presents and I would like to thank them also for all the nice things they have said about me."

Our picture shows (left to right) Keith Worsley, Steve Norton, Castleford R.L. Queen Noreen Dale and skipper Brian Lockwood.

Four

The Reilly Years
1975-1987

Reilly's future is with Cas

By **ARTHUR HADDOCK**

Mal Reilly, the Castleford forward, who has flown to Australia to play for Sydney club Manly-Warringha, will be returning to Wheldon Road in October to take up a long-term contract with them as player-coach.

Castleford chairman Mr. Phil Brunt said today: "He is the world's best forward and a lot of effort has been put in to clinch his return to Wheldon Road permanently.

"I hope Castleford people realise what an important move this is for the club, and show their appreciation by making the turnstiles click."

Reilly (27), returned to Castleford just after the start of this season to play with them and lifted their fortunes considerably, although his appearances became restricted by a knee injury.

£15,000 DEAL

He signed the Castleford contract before flying out with his wife and family to fulfil the last part of his agreement with Manly, who paid £15,000 for him in February, 1971.

Mal Reilly signs on the dotted line, and watching to make sure there are no slip-ups on his contract to return to Castleford are club chairman Phil Brunt (seated front) and at the back (left to right) Trevor Briggs, John Walker, who is taking over as coach, Dennis Hartley, and "physio" John Malpass.

As this *Yorkshire Evening Post* headline from their 12 March 1975 edition tells us, Malcolm Reilly is back at Castleford. After a very successful spell in Australia with the Manly Sea Eagles, Reilly, pictured sitting alongside club chairman Phil Brunt, signs on the dotted line of a contract to become the club's new player-coach.

MEET THE MEN BEHIND THE SCENES

John Sheridan, 'A' Team Coach   *Dennis Hartley, 'Colts' Team Coach*   *Johnny Malpass, Physiotherapist*   *Albert Lunn, Head Groundsman*

Frank Whitehead,
Asst. Physiotherapist   *Stan Bolstridge, Masseur*   *Johnny Walker, Coaching Assistant*   *Dennis Tiffany, Secretary*

Our grateful thanks are also due to Graham Hepinstall, the under-17 team coach, and Doreen Martin, Assistant Secretary, of whom photographs were not available at the time of going to press . . . . although in Doreen's case we do not feel our printing could do justice to her beauty!

19

Castleford produced a pictorial guidebook for the 1975/76 season, containing photographs and pen pictures of the playing staff. The booklet also featured some of the unsung heroes at the club, namely the men behind the scenes. These individuals gave valuable support and loyalty to their club and it was good to see them featuring alongside the players, who are generally the ones in the spotlight.

Castleford brought Geoff Wraith back from a spell in club rugby in Australia in 1975 and he proved a very astute capture. He was an excellent full-back on attack and defence who went on to play in over 200 matches for the club. Wraith is pictured here in action against his previous English club Wakefield Trinity.

Another major signing for the club in 1975/76 season was that of stand-off Bruce Burton from Halifax, for what at the time was a very big fee of £8,000. It was unusual for Castleford to go into the market for a half-back as they had an excellent record in producing them locally. Burton, however, was an exceptional talent who could turn a match round. His career was unfortunately cut short through injury, but not before lighting up many a match as well as scoring 89 tries and 45 goals in just 135 matches for Cas.

The 1976/77 season was a big one for Castleford as they won two trophies in the No. 6 and the BBC Floodlit competitions. In the Players final at Salford they faced Blackpool, in what was one of the biggest days in the Seasiders history. Cas were odds-on favourites to take the trophy, but Blackpool gave them the fright of their lives before eventually succumbing to a 25-15 defeat. In the Floodlit Trophy, Leigh were defeated 12-4 in a bruising encounter.

Scrum-half Gary Stephens races away from the Blackpool Borough cover in the 1977 Players No. 6 final. A 1979 Great Britain tourist, Gary Stephens was another excellent locally-produced half-back. He made 272 appearances for Cas before a big money transfer to Wigan, the reported £35,000 deal being the highest transfer fee that the club had ever received.

With gallant Blackpool finally defeated, player-coach Malcolm Reilly collects the Players No. 6 Trophy alongside ace kicker Geoff 'Sammy' Lloyd and long-serving hooker Bob Spurr, as their colleagues collect their winners' medals. It was Castleford's first time in the final of this competition, which was the forerunner of the Regal Trophy.

Time to relax a little as the champagne flows in the dressing room. A battle-scarred Bob Spurr looks happy as John Joyner and full-back Geoff Wraith keep their hands on the Players Trophy. Kneeling down is Aussie prop forward Paul Khan and 'sharing' Steve Fenton's bubbly is Bruce Burton.

PLAYER'S No 6 · RUGBY LEAGUE

Players No. 6 Trophy 1976-77
Celebration Dinner

Winners Castleford
Runner-up Blackpool Borough

Losing Semi-finalists Leigh-Widnes

Menu

Ham and Pea Soup

Goujon of Plaice

Half Roasted Spring Chicken
with Chamberton Sauce

Potatoes and Vegetables

Gateaux

Programme

Loyal Toast

Players No. 6 Trophy Awards
presented by Mr B. H. Wray
Marketing and Sales Director
John Player & Sons

Response by Mr H. Womersley
Chairman Rugby Football League

Wine

St. Emilion

Macon Villages

Dancing to Allan Wood Band
D.R.M. Disco

An impressive programme of events as winners and losers joined together for the 1976/77 Players No. 6 celebration dinner and dance. No doubt a jolly good time was had by all.

63

Castleford had been runners-up on four occasions in the Yorkshire County Cup, but the trophy eluded them until 1977. They went into the final at Headingley against Featherstone as the underdogs, but turned the form book inside out, with a victory that was more convincing than the 17-7 scoreline suggests. The Man of the Match award went to Bruce Burton, but the pack, which contained a number of unsung heroes, laid the platform. Jubilant skipper Malcolm Reilly holds the trophy aloft, to the delight of Alf Weston, Geoff Wraith, Bob Spurr, Geoff Lloyd and John Joyner.

Having won the Yorkshire Cup, the rest of the campaign in 1977/78 was a mixed bag. In the Challenge Cup amateurs Pilkingtons Recs gave Cas a massive scare by holding them to a single point victory in round one. In the second round it took two replays before Workington were ousted, only for Cas to then fall at Featherstone in the quarter-final. From left to right, back row: Tony Fisher, Geoff Lloyd, Malcolm Reilly, Geoff Wraith, John Joyner, Alan Dickinson. Front row: Alf Weston, Clive Pickerill, Graham Tyreman, Terry Richardson, Bruce Burton, Steve Fenton, Phil Johnson.

The team line-up before a Challenge Cup second round match against Dewsbury in March 1979. Cas won 31-15, but the following week St Helens ended their cup dreams at the quarter-final stage. From left to right, back row: Jimmy Crampton, John Joyner, Paul Orr, Geoff Wraith, David Finch, Mal Reilly, Brian Hughes, Derek Woodall, George Claughton. Front row: Steve Fenton, Bob Spurr, Gary Stephens, Bruce Burton, Phil Johnson, Terry Richardson.

Paul Orr in action against Wigan in the John Player competition, 29 October 1979. Orr was a local junior product but turned professional with Salford and then had a spell with Keighley before returning to his roots. He also had a spell as Academy coach with Cas and one player who emerged from that time was his son Danny, who has gone on to establish himself as a present day star.

The full line-up that took on Wigan in that 1979 John Player match and won 24-10 was, from left to right, back row: Sid Huddlestone, George Ballantyne, Gary Connell, Geoff Wraith, David Finch, Kevin Ward, Paul Orr, Keith Worsley. Front row: Jimmy Crampton, Ian Birkby, Gary Hyde, John Joyner, Bob Spurr, George Claughton, Steve Fenton.

Andy Timson races through the York defence in this Yorkshire Cup second round tie at Castleford in August 1981. Cas progressed to the semi-finals in a high scoring encounter by 42 points to 30. Timson, who scored a hat-trick in the match, was a very exiting young loose forward who won Great Britain Under-24 caps against France in 1982. Unfortunately, injuries blighted his career and he was unable to truly fulfil his early promise.

Gary Hyde attacks the Bradford Northern defence in the 1981 Yorkshire Cup final at Headingley. Cas had easily overcome Batley at the semi-final stage with a performance that should have brought a far more convincing scoreline than the eventual 10-5 and they defeated Bradford to take the cup for the second time in their history. Jack Bentley, writing in the *Daily Express*, summed the match up well, stating that 'Northern won the scrums but in everything else they were left wallowing in the wake of high speed Cas'.

Fans and players join together to celebrate Castleford's fine Yorkshire Cup win in 1981. Both teams went into the final in poor form, with Bradford slight favourites. Thankfully the bookies got it wrong.

Man of the Match Barry Johnson with his well-deserved award, alongside his captain John Joyner and the trophy after the 1981 Yorkshire Cup final. Johnson was a top-class ball-handling prop whose outstanding potential brought the unwelcome attention of dubious tactics by some opponents.

Player-coach Malcolm Reilly on his way to a try against Hull in the 1982 Challenge Cup semi-final at Headingley. Hull's full-back Gary Kemble was unable to cover in time, whilst former Cas star Steve Norton can only look on. Unfortunately, this was the only Castleford try as they went down 11-15. It was the first of three heartbreaking semi-final defeats at the hands of Hull in four seasons. In 1983 Hull triumphed 14-7 and in 1985, in a replay, 22-16, after a 10-10 draw in the first clash.

Jimmy Crampton in the semi-final against Hull in March 1982. Crampton actually joined Cas from Hull as part of the exchange deal that took Steve Norton to the Boulevard. In the background is a young Lee Crooks, who was later to move in the opposite direction, via Leeds.

Another Challenge Cup semi-final and another clash with Hull, this time in 1983. Barry Higgins is the player taking the ball forward for Castleford at Elland Road, but his team were defeated 7-14 as the Humbersiders once again marched on to Wembley.

KENT INVICTA
Rugby League Football Club

Sponsored by
WIMPEY HOMES

The Rugby League
STATE EXPRESS
CHALLENGE CUP

FIRST ROUND

KENT INVICTA
V
CASTLEFORD

SATURDAY FEBRUARY 11th 1984
KICK-OFF 2.15 P.M.

OFFICIAL PROGRAMME 50p

LONDON ROAD STADIUM, MAIDSTONE, KENT.

SEASON
1983/84

In 1983 a new club entered the rugby league. Kent Invicta were based in Maidstone and this step to introduce a new side far away from the code's traditional heartland was greeted by some as the possible start of an expansion programme. Sadly, the club lasted just one season at Maidstone and one more, after a relocation, as Southend Invicta. In the 1984 Challenge Cup Castleford were drawn to play against Kent in Maidstone and their one and only journey into the 'Garden of England' was a productive one, as they won the fixture.

After falling at the semi-final hurdle on those three occasions in the early eighties, Castleford eventually won a long awaited return to the Challenge Cup final in 1986. The semi-final at Central Park against Oldham was a very tough and bruising encounter, but with Man of the Match Bob Beardmore to the fore, the day was won with an 18-7 victory – Cas were back at Wembley.

The man who was to go on to be a Wembley star, Jamie Sandy. The diminutive Aborigine, in action here in the semi-final, won the hearts of Castleford supporters through the campaign. At the time Aussie players tended to guest with English clubs in their home 'off season' rather than sign longer-term contracts. Sandy came from the Easts club in Queensland and spent just the one, albeit memorable, campaign with Cas.

The semi-final is over and post-match celebrations spilled onto the playing area; four heroes of the pack – Stuart Horton, Kevin Ward, Ian French and Martin Ketteridge – have to make their way through both spectators and police on route to the dressing rooms. Stuart Horton was a talented hooker, who through the cup run deputised for the club's regular number nine Kevin Beardmore. However, Beardmore was back to fitness for the final to line up alongside his twin brother Bob, although Horton had his moment of glory with a late substitute appearance and a winners medal.

The *Yorkshire Evening Post* marked Castleford's return to Wembley after a sixteen-year gap with this special edition. Club skipper John Joyner rightly featured on the cover, as he achieved one of his goals in leading his side to the final. At the time Joyner was in his fourteenth year with the club and he had already broken the overall appearance record with quite a career still before him. Inside the content made much of the fact that coach Mal Reilly was facing his long time friend Roger Millward. Having moved to Hull as a player, the former Cas star had gone on to coach the Rovers with no little success. Now Millward was trying to plot the downfall of his hometown club in the season's biggest match.

Another one for the collectors – the 1986 Wembley programme. Silk Cut had become the competition sponsors and their distinctive style has created some interesting, if unorthodox, programme covers.

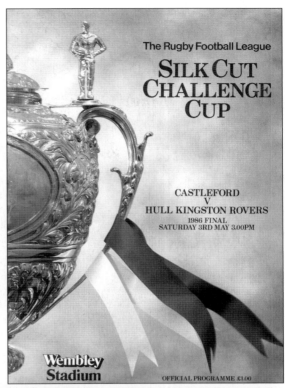

Australian loose forward Ian French breaks through the Hull KR cover in the 1986 Wembley final. French was a very influential figure in the cup campaign without making the headlines of his compatriot Jamie Sandy, who scored one of the final's great tries. Both stayed just the one season with Castleford and even had to return home between the semi-final win and the final. In the build-up to the final the duo played against each other in Brisbane for their respective clubs Wynum Manly and Easts.

Centre Tony Marchant, who scored a superb opening try in the 1986 final, makes another break through the Hull KR lines. Marchant, who was to win Test match honours, left Cas in 1989 and had a successful spell at Bradford. From Odsal he moved to Dewsbury before a brief return to his hometown club in the twilight of his career.

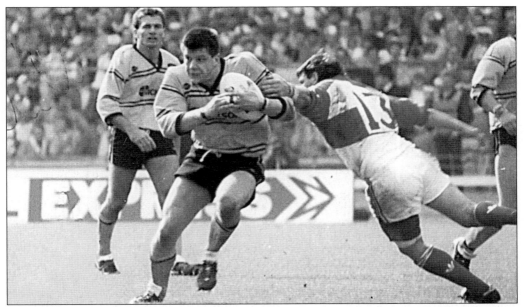

Second rower Martin Ketteridge breaks free from Gavin Miller's tackle in the 1986 Wembley final. Ketteridge was a hard-working forward and goal-kicker who notched 18 goals in the cup campaign.

John Joyner lifts the 1986 Challenge Cup after his side's thrilling 15-14 victory in front of an 82,000 Wembley crowd. Having looked to have the match sewn up, Cas were rocked by Hull's late fightback and had to endure the agony of a last minute try which, had it been converted, would have given Rovers the cup. Thankfully the reliable John Dorahy, nicknamed 'Joe Cool', missed, what was in truth a difficult kick and Castleford triumphed. The general consensus at the time was that it would have been 'robbery' had the kick been successful, such was the dominance of Joyner and his men for most of the eighty minutes. Alongside Joyner clutching his medal and the cup's plinth, is the Lance Todd Trophy winner, Bob Beardmore. The scrum-half scored a try, following through on his own kick, and also what was to prove the decisive point with a drop goal in a typically busy display.

Happiness is etched all over the face of Keith 'Beefy' England as he joins his colleagues on the traditional lap of honour around Wembley Stadium after the 1986 final.

Where did you get that hat? Prop forward Barry Johnson enjoys his opportunity to lift the cup. It seemed at the time that the players were never going to return to the dressing rooms as they enjoyed posing with the cup well beyond the final whistle.

The *Pontefract and Castleford Express* celebrated Castleford's Wembley triumph with a special edition of their newspaper. 'Classy Cas' was an appropriate phrase, but inside there were reflections on the ultimate closeness of the match and those last minute worries as well as the views of the personalities, on and off the field, who had been involved. Skipper John Joyner said that it was the best feeling in his life and club chairman David Poulter said that he knew that the team would do it. As is often the case with politicians, local MP Geoff Lofthouse didn't miss the opportunity to make a point when he congratulated the team on 'being able to put on a national spectacular from a small mining town, which has been devastated by the government's economic policy'.

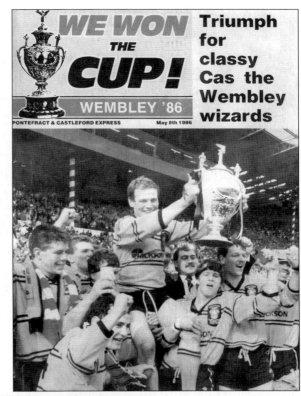

The usual formal shot with the 1986 cup winners lined up alongside board members and club secretary Denise Cackett. David Poulter is the proud chairman whilst coach Malcolm Reilly and his assistant Dave Sampson line up to the right of the front row. The players from the final, minus the departed Aussies are, from left to right, back row: Stuart Horton, Keith England, Barry Johnson, Gary Lord, Martin Ketteridge, Gary Hyde, David Plange, Kevin Ward, David Roockley. Front row: Tony Marchant, John Joyner, Bob Beardmore, Kevin Beardmore.

Brothers in arms Kevin and Bob Beardmore pose with the Challenge Cup on the roof of the Castleford Civic Centre at the 1986 homecoming. Both could be proud of the part that they played in winning the cup and of the service that they gave to Castleford.

Time to share in the celebrations: the 1986 Wembley heroes returned home to a massive welcome as thousands of the club's followers once again lined the streets and at the Civic Centre, where a reception was being held. Many supporters who had spent the night in London following the final had dashed back to Castleford for another glimpse of the cup. The Wallace Arnold double-decker with players and officials on board was, as ever, the transport for the occasion.

Castleford, as cup winners, travelled to the Isle of Man prior to the 1986/87 season to face the previous year's champions Halifax in the Charity Shield. Halifax triumphed 9-8 before a crowd of 3,276. This trophy was contested for four years on the Isle of Man before being switched to the mainland and then, ultimately, abandoned.

Two of the club's Australian signings for 1986/87, Colin Scott and Bret Atkins. Scott was a Queensland representative full-back but fitted in well at centre whilst Atkins, who played for Canberra back home, was a second rower. He had a previous spell with Cas in 1983/84 and his return was very popular with the club's followers who took to his strong running style.

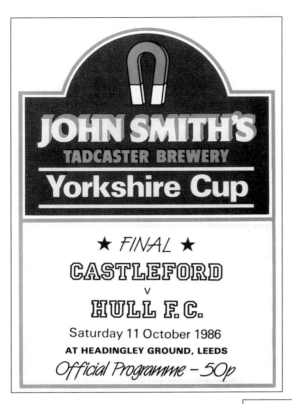

JOHN SMITH'S
TADCASTER BREWERY
Yorkshire Cup

★ *FINAL* ★

CASTLEFORD
v
HULL F.C.

Saturday 11 October 1986
AT HEADINGLEY GROUND, LEEDS
Official Programme – 50p

Still fresh from their Wembley triumph, Castleford were soon back on the cup trail in 1986/87. They defeated Halifax in round one and then thrashed local rivals Leeds 38-16 and Featherstone 30-2 in rounds two and three to reach the Yorkshire Cup final. Having defeated Hull KR at Wembley in 1986, their Yorkshire Cup final opponents were Hull.

Another Man of the Match award for the Beardmores. This time it is hooker Kevin's turn as he clutches the trophy following the 1986 Yorkshire Cup final at Headingley when he scored two tries. Castleford defeated Hull 31-24 in a real thriller. The win was seen as some revenge for the heartbreaking semi-final defeats suffered against the Humberside outfit in the first half of the decade.

St George player Chris Johns was another Australian guest with Cas for the 1986/87 campaign. Johns was a classy centre who scored a tremendous try on his debut against Halifax. He went on to great success with Brisbane and Australia but spent just the one season with Castleford.

Off the field the Aussie guests did their share of work in the community. At the time many of the British players were still part-time rugby players and had jobs to go to during the day. The Australians, on the other hand, were full-time and as such were available to, for example, spend time in local schools coaching youngsters. Here, Chris Johns is pictured taking his turn.

Some very good Australian players had guested with Castleford, but the capture of rising international star Bob Lindner in 1986 was a real coup. Before Lindner could link up with his new colleagues he had to complete his international duties as a member of the Kangaroo's touring party. In the first two Test matches, at Old Trafford and Elland Road, Lindner was in direct opposition to two of his soon-to-be team-mates, Tony Marchant and Kevin Ward, who were key players in the Great Britain line-up. Lindner's Aussies had very much the upper hand with a 38-16 success in Manchester and a more emphatic 34-4 victory in Leeds. Lindner was a tryscorer in that Second Test and also in the third – by which time Tony Marchant had lost his British place but Kevin Ward kept his in a much improved, but still losing, British performance. His tour commitments limited Lindner's Castleford appearances to just nine, but he showed enough class to be brought back for a second, although less successful, stint in 1987.

Castleford kicked off their 1987/88 campaign with a trip to France to face Halifax. The French club Albi had invited these two English clubs, as winners of the main prizes from the previous year, to take part in an exhibition match in June at their stadium in France. Both were happy to oblige and, as the poster proclaims, it was game on.

The trip to Albi proved to be a successful one as Castleford won the match against Halifax 26-6. The Cas boys celebrate – mainly in the Halifax colours after an exchange of jerseys – on winning the match and the magnificent trophy that went with it.

Bob Lindner and Michael Beattie, two of Castleford's Aussie signings for the 1987/88 campaign, pose before the Yorkshire Cup final against Bradford at Headingley. The match ended in a 12-12 draw, but Bradford clinched the replay, another tough encounter, 11-2.

For the 1987/88 season, former player and assistant coach Dave Sampson had taken over the senior role from Mal Reilly, who had been awarded the Great Britain coaching job. Although finishing in a creditable seventh place in the league, it was a mixed campaign and Sampson left the club after the one term. However, this was the season that Dave's son Dean Sampson made his Cas debut and he continues to serve the club superbly to this day. The line-up features, from left to right, back row: Chris Chapman, David Rookley, Kevin Ward, David Plange, John Fifita, Dean Sampson, Bob Lindner, Kevin Beardmore, Roy Southernwood. Front row: Keith England, Michael Beattie, Tony Marchant, John Joyner, Bob Beardmore, Giles Boothroyd, Wayne Thornton.

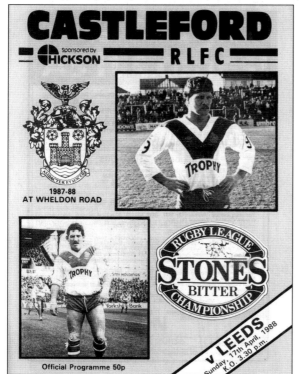

Kevin Beardmore and Kevin Ward featured in their international jerseys on the cover of the club programme for this April 1988 local derby against Leeds. Always one of the season's highlights, Castleford, who take great delight in putting one over their big city neighbours, won this encounter 26-12. Beardmore and Ward both represented their country in the Test matches against France that year and secured places in the Great Britain tour party for the summer 1988 tour of Papua, Australia and New Zealand.

Five
The Australian Influence
1988-1993

Never regarded as big spenders, Castleford started to splash out into the transfer market in the late 1980s. The club set a new world record transfer fee when they bought Graham Steadman at a cost of £175,000 from near neighbours Featherstone Rovers in 1989. Steadman was from the town but started his professional career with York before a move to Featherstone. Despite receiving that huge transfer fee, Rovers fans were extremely bitter when their star player was transferred to their arch rivals. Steadman, shown here in action for Great Britain, proved a tremendous buy for Castleford as his record of 121 tries and 182 goals in 237 appearances testifies.

An Australian coach, in the form of Darryl Van de Velde, marked a big change in Castleford's outlook when he joined the club in 1988. A confident forthright character, Van de Velde had achieved some success in the Queensland competition and was eager to repeat that in England. His impact was immediate and, whilst doing things differently to the way that the club had been used to, his keenness to shake off its 'small town' image made him very popular with the club's followers. Here Van de Velde, typically with his headphones, sits alongside club chairman David Poulter.

Darryl Van de Velde inherited most of this squad who represented the club in his first season, 1988/89, but he did bring in a couple of highly rated Australian signings in Ronnie Gibbs and Gary Belcher. From left to right, back row: Martin Ketteridge, Keith England, Chris Chapman, Kenny Hill, Roy Southernwood, Ron Gibbs. Middle row: David Poulter (chairman), Gary Belcher, Kevin Ward, Grant Anderson, Giles Boothroyd, Dean Sampson, Mick Morgan (assistant coach). Front row: Darryl Van de Velde, David Plange, Bob Beardmore, John Joyner, Kevin Beardmore, David Roockley, Tony Marchant.

Castleford versus Huddersfield in the Yorkshire Cup first round match in September 1988. David Plange was one of three Cas players to record try hat-tricks as their side won by a massive 94-12 – the club's highest ever score.

Gary Belcher, the Canberra Raiders and Australian Test full-back, was one of Darryl Van de Velde's first signings. Belcher was a class act, but his time at the club was short. Injuries brought an earlier than anticipated end to his season in England and he returned home having played in just 10 matches for Cas.

It wasn't long before the new coach had taken his team to potential glory with Cas reaching the 1988 Yorkshire Cup final. Leeds were the opposition at Elland Road and an impressive crowd of almost 23,000 gathered to watch these two keen rivals do battle. On the day though, Leeds proved the stronger and, despite a typically strong performance from Kevin Ward, Cas crashed 12-33 in what was regarded as one of the games of the season.

In January 1989 the Beardmore twins, Kevin and Bob, completed their well-deserved benefit year. They received what was easily a club record figure for a benefit, testimony to a lot of hard work by the organisers, but also recognition of their efforts on behalf of the club, whose supporters held them in very high esteem.

Coach Van de Velde made quite a few changes to his squad in his first term, so when his charges gathered for the pre-season photocall in 1989 there were a number of new faces on view. From left to right, back row: Martin Ketteridge, Andy Clarke, Keith England, Steve Larder, Kevin Ward. Middle row: David Poulter (chairman), Mick Morgan (assistant coach), Mark Gibson, Paul Crabtree, David Plange, Ron Gibbs, Dean Blankley, Stan Timmins (conditioner), Darryl Van de Velde. Front row: Darren Price, Tony Marchant, Grant Anderson, John Joyner, Kevin Beardmore, Shaun Irwin, Graham Steadman.

Ronnie 'Rambo' Gibbs takes on the Hunslet defence in this Yorkshire Cup first round tie in September 1989 at Elland Road. Cas won 44-0. The scoring highlight was winger David Plange's four tries in an emphatic victory over a side he was later to play for and coach. Gibbs was a very popular player in his two spells with the club. Unfortunately, he had a fiery reputation, which went before him, and referees appeared to keep a much closer watch on him than most. Often, Gibbs was far more 'sinned against than sinning'.

Sponsored by
HICKSON

CASTLEFORD

V

NEW ZEALAND

British COAL

1989 Kiwi Tour

Tuesday
3rd October 1989
Kick Off 7.30 p.m.

Official Souvenir Programme 80p

Castleford skipper John Joyner and his opposite number for the 1989 New Zealand tourists, Hugh McGahan, pose on the cover of the official programme for the club's match against the Kiwis. At one point an understrength Cas outfit were leading 20-6, but the introduction of former player Gary Freeman by New Zealand turned things around and his side scored sixteen unanswered points to snatch a victory. Two future Castleford players, Tawera Nikau and Brendon Tuuta, featured in the visitors' pack.

When Great Britain took on France in April 1990 there were four Castleford players on international duty. Before the match they posed for this photograph in their official blazers, from left to right: Kevin Beardmore, Keith England, Shaun Irwin and Graham Steadman.

Keith 'Beefy' England in action for Great Britain during that 1990 clash with France. 'Beefy' was a home-grown talent who could be relied upon to give 100 per cent whenever he played. He won junior Great Britain honours when playing for the Castleford Colts side and went on to win 11 senior Test match caps with a wholehearted approach that was appreciated by all.

In the 1990/91 season, Cas again reached the Yorkshire Cup final. They were expected to have a fairly easy ride against local rivals Wakefield at Elland Road, but the match that was much tighter than expected and they won by only three points, 11-8. The happy team with assistant coach Mick Morgan and John Walker enjoy their celebrations with a little help from the match sponsor's product.

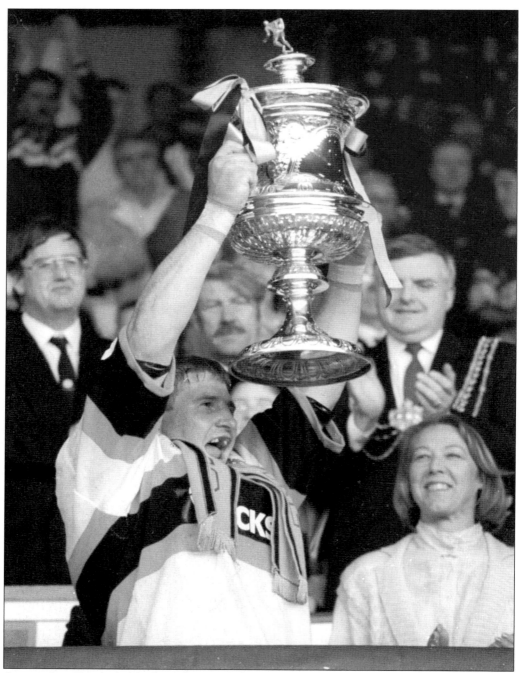

Captain Lee Crooks holds the 1990 Yorkshire Cup aloft. Another big money signing by Darryl Van de Velde, prop forward Lee Crooks joined the club in January 1990 for a £150,000 fee from Leeds. Crooks had already established himself as one of Britain's best forwards from an early age at Hull, his hometown club. His move to Leeds wasn't a great success, but at Cas he recaptured his best form and regained his international status, which ultimately won him a total of 19 Great Britain caps. Crooks made 222 appearances for Cas, scoring 18 tries and kicking 597 goals.

Back at base Castleford's Australian players, Gary French, Jeff Hardy and Steve Larder, pose with the 1970 Yorkshire Cup. Former Brisbane Broncos scrum-half French had to sit out the final through injury, but the ex-Illawarra Steelers duo of Hardy and Larder both played their part in the winning performance.

In 1990 an Australian touring party hit these shores. Three of the tourists, Bob Lindner, Gary Belcher and Chris Johns, had previously enjoyed a spell with Castleford and they were happy to pose for the cover of the club's official programme for the match against the Aussies. Belcher and Lindner played in the match and helped their countrymen to a 28-8 win over their former club.

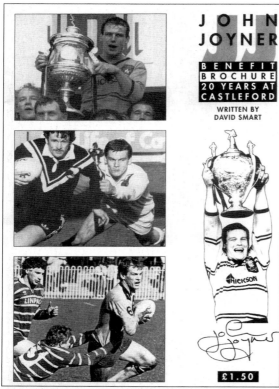

JOHN JOYNER

BENEFIT BROCHURE 20 YEARS AT CASTLEFORD

WRITTEN BY DAVID SMART

£1.50

John Joyner enjoyed a tremendous career with the Castleford club and after twenty years celebrated with a well-deserved benefit. His tally of over 600 appearances is the highest made by anyone in the club's history and he also went on to fill the coach's role for a spell. On the representative front no one has made more appearances for Great Brtain whilst a Cas player than John's 16 caps and he also represented England on 4 occasions and Yorkshire 12 times.

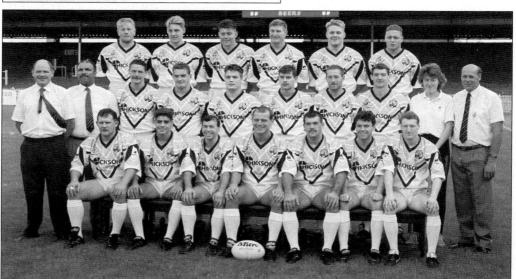

The squad pose on the eve of what was to prove another thrilling and rewarding campaign in 1991/92. From left to right, back row: Neil Roebuck, Andy Hay, Martin Ketteridge, Lee Crooks, Dean Sampson, St John Ellis. Middle row: Mick Morgan, Stan Timmins (conditioner), Graham Steadman, Shaun Irwin, Graham Southernwood, Tony Smith, Gary Atkins, Grant Anderson, Bernadette Scatchard (physiotherapist), Darryl Van de Velde. Front row: Kevin Beardmore, Jon Wray, Paul Fletcher, John Joyner, Keith England, Mike Ford, Simon Middleton.

As well as their Australian imports, Castleford had some top-class New Zealand stars in their ranks during the 1990s. None were better than international loose forward Tawera Nikau, who was persuaded to join Cas before the start of the 1991/92 term in the face of tremendous competition from clubs at home and abroad. Nikau is featured here with the Yorkshire Cup after his side's victory over Bradford in October 1991, having captained his side in the absence of injured regular skipper Lee Crooks. The highly popular Kiwi played in 165 matches for Cas before switching to Australia with the Cronulla Sharks in 1996.

The jubilant Castleford squad in celebratory mood at Elland Road after they had retained the Yorkshire Cup in 1991 with what was a very comfortable 28-6 victory over Bradford. Full-back Graham Steadman took the individual honours with a record-breaking cup final tally of 16 points (from 2 tries and 4 goals) but the whole side performed well in this runaway success. Having taken fifty-one years to win this cup for the first time, it was becoming a regular feature in the Castleford trophy cabinet.

Graham Steadman struggles to break free from the Widnes defence in this October 1991 encounter. Cas lost this home match 20-22 but generally fared well in the league and ended the campaign in third place in Division One. By this time Steadman, who had joined the club as a stand-off, had switched to the full-back position – a conversion that proved a winner.

This Rowe cartoon appeared in the official programme for the 1992 Challenge Cup semi-final when Cas defeated Hull 8-4 to reach the final at Wembley. Hull were Castleford's bogey side at this stage of the competition in the 1980s and they were dogged opponents in this clash. Of the two Australian coaches it was Castleford's Darryl Van de Velde who was smiling as his charges triumphed over Noel Cleal's Hull to set up a final clash with Wigan.

Action from the 1992 Challenge Cup semi-final featuring the Man of the Match Graeme Bradley. The Aussie was signed from Penrith as a centre but another astute positional switch by Darryl Van de Velde saw Bradley move to the second row where he showed his best form.

Tony Smith was called into the side for the Challenge Cup semi-final against Hull as a late replacement for the injured Ritchie Blackmore. He was a key figure in his side's only try with a break and then a perfect pass that enabled the supporting Mike Ford to score.

The 1992 Challenge Cup final against Wigan saw Castleford suffer their first defeat at the famous stadium. Wigan had taken the trophy in the previous four years and were in no mood to relinquish it (and indeed didn't for another four years). Cas were hit with early points and although they rallied a little in the second half they never looked like wresting control and went down 12-28. At the time, though, that was no disgrace as Wigan were sweeping the board and in their semi-final had thrashed Bradford 71-10. Here, Mike Ford, who was in his first season at the club after a £77,500 switch from Oldham, kicks for position.

Dean Sampson was a thirty-third minute substitute for injured skipper Lee Crooks in the 1992 Wembley final defeat. Dean is well held here by a Wigan defender, but over the years he has proved very difficult to contain by the opposition in a marvellous career with Castleford. By the close of the century he had amassed over 350 appearances for his only club and, despite not gaining as many representative honours that Cas followers feel he deserves, he has represented both England and Great Britain.

Wing star St John Ellis strides out against Warrington in this 1993 clash. A bargain buy from York, 'Singe' was a real crowd pleaser who developed into a Great Britain international at Castleford.

The club were changing their programme cover on an annual basis and this is the style in 1992/93: Mike Ford is the cover star. As the season drew to a close, coach Darryl Van de Velde announced that he was leaving the club and returning to Australia to take over as chief executive of the newly formed Queensland Crushers. Cas wasted little time in announcing his successor as John Joyner, the long serving player and club captain who had been Van de Velde's coaching assistant.

Six

Highs and Lows
Through the Nineties
1994-1999

John Joyner's first season in charge of the club in 1993/94 could hardly have gone better. The Regal Trophy was won with magnificent displays and the club were also Premiership finalists at Old Trafford and Challenge Cup semi-finalists. Here, inspirational skipper Lee Crooks is pictured breaking the Wigan cover in the Premiership final.

When Castleford reached the 1994 Regal Trophy final few people gave them any chance against Wigan, despite their impressive semi-final defeat of Bradford at Odsal. The important people though, in the form of the players and coaching staff, were confident and carried off a stunning victory. Wigan weren't just beaten – they were thrashed to the tune of 33-2 in the biggest defeat that they had ever suffered in eighty-seven major finals! This *League Express* cover captures the event in all its glory.

The Regal Trophy match programme provides an excellent souvenir of a memorable day in Castleford's history. Summing up in his *Yorkshire Post* match report, Ray Fletcher says it all: 'Never have such hot favourites been beaten so comprehensively in a big match as the champions were against Castleford in the Regal Trophy final at Headingley on Saturday.'

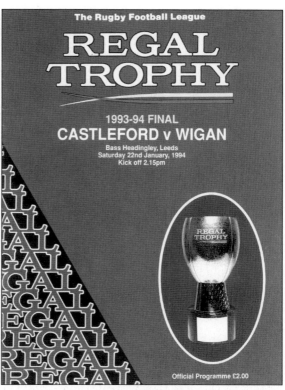

Second row forward Ian Smales, like so many of his colleagues, turned in one of the best performances of his career in the Regal Trophy final. In this shot, Smales is about to face Wigan's tough prop Kelvin Skerrett.

Tony Morrison faces the full force of the Wigan defence in this shot from the Regal final. It was worth the knocks though for the former Swinton back rower, who was another hero at Headingley, when he collected his winners' medal.

A delighted Lee Crooks lifts the 1994 Regal Trophy. As captain, Lee had set a magnificent example to his charges throughout the match. His 16-point haul was an individual record total in the final and his six goals (out of six kicks) equalled the final record. It was fitting that his try was the last of the game and, although by then the match was well won, it was a cracker.

The Regal Trophy Man of the Match winner Martin Ketteridge proudly holds the prize that he had played such a big part in winning. Ketteridge, who has Tony Morrison alongside him, served Cas for many years as a good goal-kicker and a strong running, consistent performer in the pack. The 1994 Regal final was his finest hour and he certainly chose the right moment to play what many people felt to be the game of his career.

Celebrations all round for the 1994 Regal Trophy winners as they pause during their lap of honour around the Headingley pitch.

Having suffered defeat in the Challenge Cup semi-final, Castleford were making another bid for a second final appearance of the year, this time in the Premiership. The semi-final took them to Odsal to face Bradford. The pack set a good lead with Tawera Nikau, pictured in action during the match, and Lee Crooks working well. Eventually, Cas proved too strong for Bradford and with a 24-16 scoreline won a place in the Old Trafford final to meet Wigan.

Wigan had gained some revenge for their Regal Trophy final defeat by knocking Castleford off the Challenge Cup trail at the semi-final stage. The Premiership final was to offer them another opportunity. It was an opportunity that they took – but not before Cas had fought back to cut a sixteen-point deficit to just four. However, despite being pressed to the end, Wigan were able to hold on and claimed a 24-20 victory.

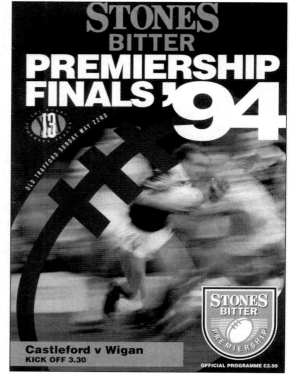

A crowd of 35,644 gathered at Manchester United's Old Trafford ground for the 1994 Premiership final. In a real thriller, Castleford's hooker and former Wigan player Richard Russell moves the ball out to the supporting Dean Sampson.

St John Ellis takes on Wigan in the Premiership final. 'Singe' was unable to cross the tryline in the match, but in the season scored a club record 40 tries. Keith Howe's previous record of 36 touchdowns had stood for 30 years before the popular Ellis overtook it with 2 tries against Wakefield in April 1994.

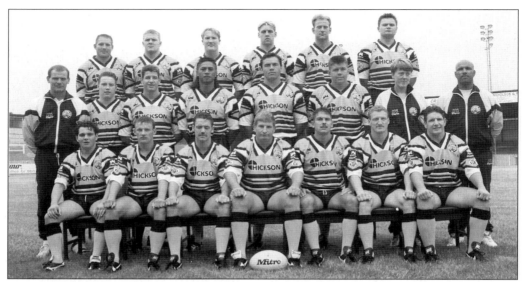

Hopes were high of another good campaign in 1994/95, despite having lost two star men, Mike Ford and St John Ellis, at the close of the previous term. Both had opted to join their former coach Darryl Van de Velde in Australia with the Queensland Crushers. This squad lined up for the pre-season photocall, from left to right, back row: Ian Smales, Dean Sampson, Nathan Sykes, Andy Hay, Richard Goddard, Tony Kemp. Middle row: John Joyner (coach), Jason Flowers, Tony Morrison, Tawera Nikau, Ritchie Blackmore, Martin Ketteridge, Bernadette Scatchard (physiotherapist), Stan Timmins (conditioner). Front row: Gareth Stephens, Chris Smith, Graham Steadman, Lee Crooks, Tony Smith, Simon Middleton, Richard Russell.

Season 1994/95 saw another tour of England by Australia and Cas were given a match against the Aussies. Kiwi stand-off Tony Kemp, featured in this shot from the game, had a good match but his side, although battling hard, didn't have enough in their armoury to stop the tourists.

Youngster Paul Darley came on as a second half substitute for Cas in their match against the 1994 Aussie tourists, but the damage had already been done with the visitors already eighteen points clear on their way to a 38-12 victory.

Dean Sampson struggles with the Wigan defenders in the 1994/95 Regal Trophy semi-final clash at Central Park. The defence of the trophy ended at this stage. Having defeated Wigan so well in the previous year's final, it was revenge time for the Riversiders. They ensured that there was to be no repeat and no second final for Castleford with an emphatic 34-6 win.

Cas boss bides his time

CASTLEFORD chairman Eddie Ashton is playing a canny waiting game.

He wants to see how the Featherstone and Wakefield Trinity public vote before making up his mind how to play the Wheldon Road cards.

"Castleford want to stand alone," said Ashton. "There would have been no problems if the Super League proposals had been left as that.

"But if we have to amalgamate we believe that as the most successul of the sides we should have a greater say."

Ashton revealed that he will put the club's situation to a shareholders meeting, although he was not prepared to say when the meeting will be staged.

"It'll be up to the shareholders once they have heard all the facts to decide what the club does," said Ashton, who took over as chairman a little over a year ago.

CALDER - THE MUDDY RIVER

STEVE Wagner, the Featherstone Rovers chairman, has conceded that the Post Office Road club is in turmoil as it tries to decide its future.

He has laid on the line to his club's fans that they have until just April 28th to make up their minds.

Said Wagner: "As a members' club it is only they who can ultimately decide which way Rovers go from here.

"A letter explaining the situation, together with voting slips, will go out to the members after Easter and I would urge them to return them no later than April 27th."

Wagner believes that on realistic grounds Rovers have no other choice than to go in with their old rivals to form a Super League club.

"People should know that the £100,000 on offer to first division clubs will last Rovers no longer than a month with the current debt situation," he said.

"A couple of committeemen have guaranteed the overdraft at the bank, and they will want that back soon.

"Currently the club is in debt to the tune of £400,000, and that couldn't go on, even if we wanted to stay the same as we are now.

"An answer has to come forward so that we can go to the League on May 4th to say whether we are in or out.

"I've just got a terrible feeling that the members will vote to stay out of a merger and take a risk on staying in the first division.

"From my point of view amalgamation looks the best option, but I would just urge the 1,140 members to vote with their heads and not their hearts."

● WAKEFIELD Trinity chairman Ted Richardson is so convinced that amalgamation is the way forward that he is prepared to walk voluntarily into the lions' dens

Nigel Wright

called Castleford and Featherstone.

He explained: "When I went to a public meeting of the Trinity fans I would have said that 75 per cent were against the idea.

"But you've got to sell the idea. Once I had sat down I would have said 95 per cent had changed their minds. They could see the exciting possibilities offered by this project.

"This is the best chance we've ever had to spread the game over the world, never mind just outside Yorkshire.

"I'm convinced that if the fans heard the facts and what could be achieved that they would back us all the way.

"To that end I'm prepared to go to any meeting with Castleford and Featherstone fans to put my case.

"If they'll listen, and give me a fair hearing, I'm sure that they would come round to my way of thinking and see what an exciting future amalgamation offers this area.

"If people want to stay in the first division I'll give them all the help I can.

"But it would be wasted effort.

"Many people started to understand when I took some players to a meeting and asked Nigel Wright: 'Would you stay and play if we didn't go in the Super League?'

"His answer was 'No' and that opened a few eyes."

Trinity's shareholders' are expected to give their directors the go-ahead to merge with the other two clubs at their annual meeting tomorrow.

As this *League Express* story outlines, an almighty row broke out in the spring of 1995. The formation of a Super League had been proposed and with it a switch to summer rugby and – the biggest issue of all for Castleford – a number of proposed mergers. One of these was to bring Castleford, Featherstone and Wakefield together into one merged Super League team. Shock waves understandably ran through the local community.

Protests followed the Super League proposals and these were particularly strong in the Castleford and Featherstone area. Eventually the league chiefs had a rethink and the mergers were taken off the agenda. The top ten teams in the league, plus London and Paris, were given the twelve coveted Super League spaces. Having ended the season in third place in the Division One, Castleford rightly won a place of their own in the new set up, whilst Featherstone just missed out. Wakefield lost their chance after finishing in the bottom four.

110

The 1995/96 term was to be a shortened one to allow for the switch to Super League and summer rugby in 1996. Coach John Joyner and his staff lined up with these players for the new campaign. From left to right, back row: Simon Price, Brendon Tuuta, Andrew Schick, Nathan Sykes, Lee Harland, Graham Steadman, Richard Goddard. Middle row: Paul Darley, Ian Smales, Dean Sampson, Phil Eden, Colin Maskill, Tony Smith, Andy Hill. Front row; Jason Flowers, Gareth Stephens, Simon Middleton, Lee Crooks, Chris Smith, Adrian Flynn, Tony Marchant.

Brendon Tuuta in action against Leeds in 1995/96, the code's centenary season. A New Zealand international, Tuuta had played in Australia and had a number of years with Featherstone. It broke a few hearts down Post Office Road when he joined Cas.

After all the build-up, Super League kicked off for Castleford on 31 March 1996 with a defeat against Bradford. The squad for the 1996 campaign was, from left to right, back row: Brendon Tuuta, Nathan Sykes, Adrian Flynn, Ian Smales, Andrew Schick, Lee Harland, Richard Goddard, Grant Anderson, Frano Botica. Middle row: John Lupton (groundsman), Stan Timmins (conditioner), Richard Russell, Jason Flowers, Jamie Coventry, Colin Maskill, Graham Steadman, Tony Smith, Gary Stephens (assistant coach). Front row: Gareth Stephens, Chris Smith, Dean Sampson, John Joyner, Lee Crooks, Simon Middleton, Richard Gay.

The Paris experiment lasted just two Super League campaigns before the French side called it a day. In this 1996 match against Paris St Germain, Castleford's Australian three-quarter David Chapman races away from Patrick Entat.

This picture shows the new coach Stuart Raper. Castleford had not performed particularly well in the opening Super League campaign, finishing ninth in the twelve team competition, but matters got worse in 1997. After suffering a home loss in the Challenge Cup to Salford, the opening four league matches also brought defeats. The result was a mutually agreed parting of the ways with John Joyner, ending his twenty-five year stint with the club as a player and coach. Mick Morgan took the reins on a caretaker basis until a replacement coach was found and improved things a little, but when Stuart Raper arrived from Australia in April his new charges were bottom of the league with a record of played eight lost eight. The new Aussie boss was rated as one of the most promising coaches in his homeland, having worked with the Australian Under-19s and Cronulla's reserve grade. His first couple of matches in charge at Cas brought further defeats, but he was soon turning things around and with five wins and two draws in their next twelve games – relegation, which at one time had seemed inevitable, was avoided.

During Mick Morgan's short stint as caretaker coach, Cas pulled off a smart move by bringing Mike Ford back to the club as a much-needed playmaker. More new faces were brought in to help lift the club following Stuart Raper's arrival and the new look squad posed for this shot in mid-term. From left to right: Shane Flanagan (assistant coach), Lee St Hilaire, David Chapman, Adrian Vowles, Jason Lidden, Lee Harland, Brendon Tuuta, Nathan Sykes, Andrew Schick, Ian Tonks, Richard Gay, Richard Goddard, Mike Ford, Ritchie McKell, Jason Critchley, Ian Smales, Dean Sampson, Jason Flowers, Simon Middleton, Graham Steadman, Richard Russell, Brad Davis, Danny Orr, Chris Smith, Stuart Raper.

Mike Ford in action against Paris in May 1997. Ford's return to the club that year after a spell in Australia and stints with Warrington and Wakefield provided a great boost to the fight to retain a Super League place. Had Cas gone down in the 1997 campaign, they could have found themselves permanently out of the top flight.

In the midst of their 1997 relegation battle Cas found some relief in the World Club Challenge when Super League clubs each faced Australian sides, home and away, in mini groups. Castleford faced Hunter Mariners and, in the match pictured here, Perth Reds. Jason Lidden is the Cas player being brought to ground in his side's 16-24 defeat.

Young pack star Ian Tonks, again in action in the World Club Challenge against Perth. Castleford didn't win any of their four matches against the Aussie club sides – but few English teams did, with some, unlike Cas, falling to embarrassingly high scorelines.

With the relegation worries of 1997 behind him, coach Stuart Raper not surprisingly made quite a few changes to his squad for his first full campaign of 1998. His new line-up, with their new kit and shirt sponsors, from left to right, back row: Dean Sampson, Ian Tonks, Spencer Hargrave, Paul Smith, Barrie-Jon Mather, Ritchie McKell, Andrew Schick, Gael Tallec, Nathan Sykes. Middle row: Miles Haslam (physiotherapist), Michael Smith, Lee Harland, David Chapman, Jon Wells, Danny Ellison, Jamie Benn, Richard Gay, Gareth Dobson, Tony O'Brien (conditioner). Front row: Jason Flowers, Danny Orr, Adrian Vowles, Stuart Raper, Mike Ford, Graham Steadman (assistant coach), Brad Davis, Francis Maloney, Richard Russell.

The Challenge Cup gave Castleford a tremendous start to the 1998 campaign with thrilling wins over Leeds at Headingley and Bradford at Wheldon Road. In the quarter-finals Sheffield Eagles seemed to present a perfect opportunity for progress, especially in the light of those two previous victories. However, the Eagles came to Cas full of confidence and won through on route to their first ever Wembley final. Here the home front row of Ritchie McKell, Danny Orr and Dean Sampson prepare to pack down against Sheffield.

'Viva' Brad Davis – Cas followers know that you need to sing it to the Elvis song to understand the nickname. Davis was signed from Wakefield in 1997 to boost the relegation battle and was another who played a big part. The Australian half-back had been in this country for a number of years, playing for Nottingham, Huddersfield and York before his move to Wakefield. Despite not having played in the top flight before joining Cas, he took the opportunity with both hands and has been a key figure at the club.

Dean Sampson crashes past Warrington's Michael Eagar in this Super League encounter, which Cas won 23-16 at Cardiff in July 1998. The match took place in Cardiff as part of rugby's 'On the Road' programme, which was aimed at spreading the game. Within the year Eagar and Sampson were to become team-mates as the Aussie centre switched from the Wolves to the Tigers.

More action from the 1998 'On the Road' clash with Warrington in Cardiff. Skipper Mike Ford is surrounded by his jubilant team-mates after scoring the match-clinching try.

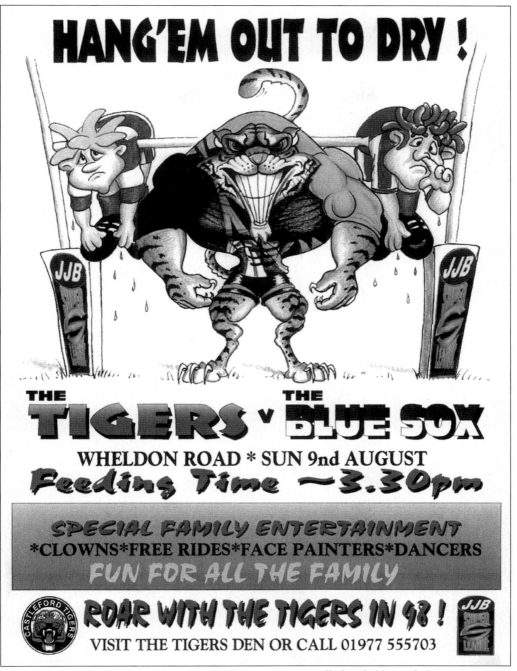

As Super League developed on the field, so activities off the field needed to grow with marketing departments taking on an ever increasing role in selling the game to a bigger audience. Amongst many initiatives, Castleford commissioned bright and amusing caricature posters by 'Mick' which were then distributed around the town to advertise forthcoming matches. This example is to promote the Halifax match in 1998 and used the visitor's nickname to good effect.

In the 1999 Super League campaign Castleford re-established themselves as a force in the game, reaching the semi-final stage in both the Challenge Cup and the Grand Final play-off. Fifth spot in the table was their best placing in the Super League and they played with a spirit and determination that won them many new friends and followers. One player who typified those qualities was local junior product Jason Flowers.

All-action club skipper Adrian Vowles in action against St Helens in the 1999 campaign.

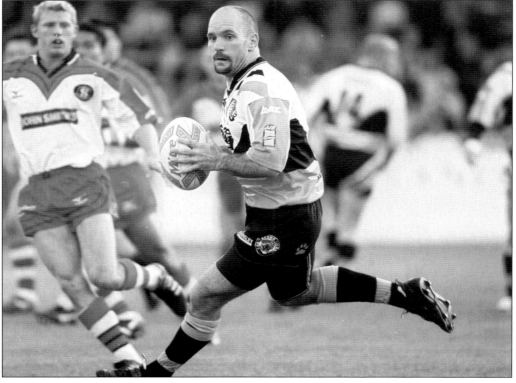

During the 1999 Challenge Cup run the Castleford team and some of the club's employees and followers became 'film stars'. The Yorkshire Media Consortium produced the film, *Taming the Tigers*, which focused on both the action and the emotions for players and followers alike as they pursued their Wembley dream. Here, Dean Sampson is being filmed and interviewed by Judi Alston, one of the film-makers.

In the new world of Super League, pre-match entertainment became very much the order of the day. As part of that entertainment Castleford started out with one mascot, but by 1999 had added another couple of 'relations'. Here we have Tigerman, Tiger Tot and Junior Tiger lining up for the camera.

Winger Darren Rogers, one of a number of new signings in 1999, led the club's tryscoring charts but couldn't escape the Salford defence on this occasion in the Challenge Cup quarter-final. Playing against his former club, Rogers scored two tries in Castleford's 30-10 victory.

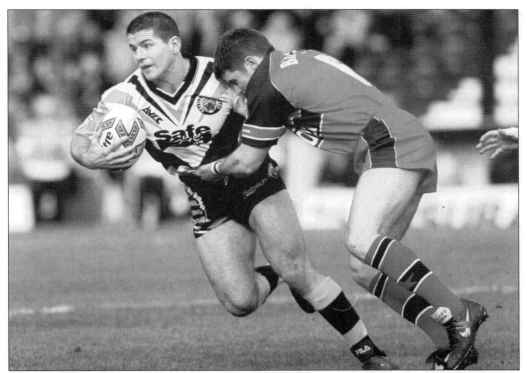

Another 1999 newcomer was Australian centre Michael Eagar, a prized capture from Warrington. He is pictured here in action against Salford in the Challenge Cup.

As the match programme proclaims, Castleford were one step away from Wembley when they reached the 1999 Challenge Cup semi-final. London Broncos were blocking the path, but they were marginal second favourites and a sixth trip to the final seemed to be on the cards.

London's Shaun Edwards stops Richard Gay in the semi-final at Headingley – as his side stopped the Tigers' ambitions. The match was regarded as a classic but that was scant consolation to the losing players and supporters. In the last ten minutes Cas took the lead, lost it, drew level and finally lost it again with just seconds remaining. The Broncos emerged winners by 33 points to 27 and the Wembley dream was over.

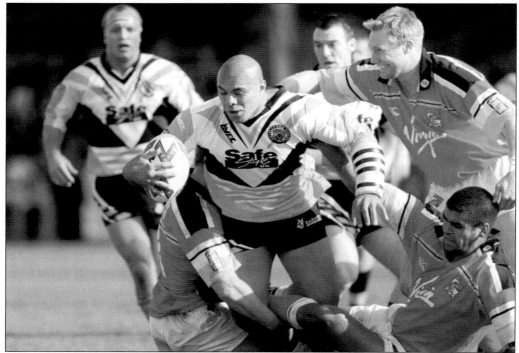

Substitute forward, Fijian James Pickering, is halted by the London defence in the 1999 Challenge Cup semi-final. Pickering had just the one season with the club and, although he came with a big reputation, injuries hampered his campaign.

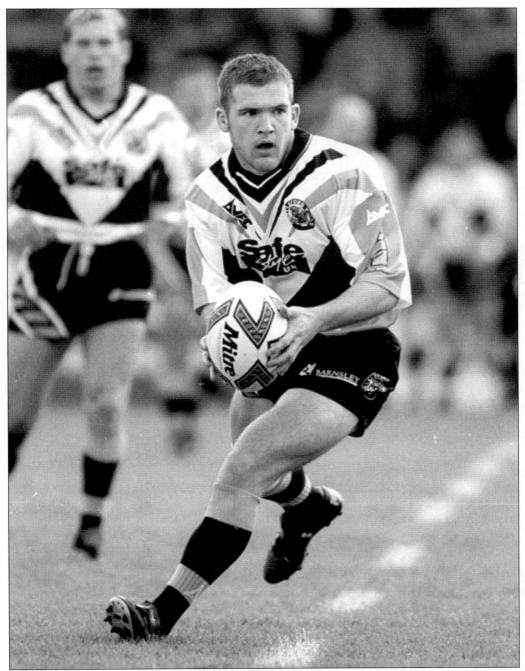

Danny Orr in action during the 1999 campaign. Danny joined the club from Kippax ARLC, who have provided Castleford with many good players and he too looks a winner. He developed through the academy set-up but established himself as a first team regular at an early age and soon won international honours with England. He is regarded as one of the game's hottest young properties and Castleford followers were delighted when he signed a long-term deal with the club in 1999.

Never one to hide his emotions after a good victory, coach Stuart Raper celebrates the clubs 1999 Super League play-off victory at Headingley over fierce local rivals Leeds Rhinos.

Castleford provided England with no less than five players for their 1999 international matches against France – Lee Harland, Darren Rogers, Nathan Sykes, Danny Orr and Dean Sampson. A sixth, Francis Maloney, left the club between the two matches. Gael Tallec, who was still at the club when the matches took place, was in the France team.

One player who epitomises the Castleford spirit and one of the very best overseas players that the club has ever signed is Adrian Vowles. Adrian capped a superb 1999 campaign when he took the game's most prestigious individual trophy in being named as the Man of Steel. Adrian had won a State of Origin appearance back home, but was surprisingly released by the North Queensland Cowboys. Their loss though was the Tigers' gain as this unassuming Aussie has proved an outstanding player and, in his capacity as club captain, an excellent leader.

Castleford's last match of the twentieth century came on Boxing Day 1999 when they played Wakefield in a friendly fixture at Wheldon Road. Both sides fielded understrength line-ups, but closed the year with an entertaining and honourable draw. Here in some of the very last Rugby League action of the century, Castleford's winger Jon Wells takes on the Wakefield defence in that Boxing Day clash.